W9-BAT-221

JAMES
BALDWIN

JAMES BALDWIN

Lisa Rosset

Senior Consulting Editor
Nathan Irvin Huggins
Director
W.E.B. Du Bois Institute for Afro-American Research
Harvard University

ST. JOHN THE BAPTIST PARISH (COUNTY) LIBRARY
1334 WEST AIRLINE HIGHWAY
LaPLACE, LOUISIANA 70068

COPY 4

CHELSEA HOUSE PUBLISHERS
New York   Philadelphia

CHELSEA HOUSE PUBLISHERS
Editor-in-Chief Nancy Toff
Executive Editor Remmel T. Nunn
Managing Editor Karyn Gullen Browne
Copy Chief Juliann Barbato
Picture Editor Adrian G. Allen
Art Director Maria Epes
Manufacturing Manager Gerald Levine

Black Americans of Achievement

Senior Editor Richard Rennert

Staff for JAMES BALDWIN
Associate Editor Perry King
Copy Editor Lisa Fenev
Deputy Copy Chief Ellen Scordato
Editorial Assistant Jennifer Trachtenberg
Picture Researcher Andrea Reithmayr
Assistant Art Director Laurie Jewell
Designer Ghila Krajzman
Production Coordinator Joseph Romano
Cover Illustration Bradford Brown

Copyright © 1989 by Chelsea House Publishers, a division of
Main Line Book Co. All rights reserved. Printed and bound in
the United States of America.

First Printing

1 3 5 7 9 8 6 4 2

Library of Congress Cataloging-in-Publication Data
   Rosset, Lisa
   James Baldwin.

   (Black Americans of achievement)
   Bibliography: p.
   Includes index.
   Summary: A biography of an American author noted for
his books on racial conflict in the United States.
   1. Baldwin, James, 1924–   —Biography—Juvenile
literature. 2. Authors, American—20th century—
Biography—Juvenile literature. 3. Civil rights workers—
United States—Biography—Juvenile literature. 4. Afro-
Americans—Civil rights—History—20th century—Juvenile
literature. [1. Baldwin, James, 1924–   .2. Authors,
American. 3. Afro-Americans—Biography] I. Title.
II. Series.
PS3532.A45Z87   1989   818'.5409 [B] [92]   88-37006
ISBN 1-55546-572-2
      0-7910-0230-6 (pbk.)

CONTENTS

—— ❦ ——

BLACK
AMERICANS
OF
ACHIEVEMENT

—•❦•—

MUHAMMAD ALI
heavyweight champion

RICHARD ALLEN
*founder of the
African Methodist
Episcopal church*

LOUIS ARMSTRONG
musician

JAMES BALDWIN
author

BENJAMIN BANNEKER
*scientist and
mathematician*

MARY MCLEOD BETHUNE
educator

BLANCHE K. BRUCE
politician

RALPH BUNCHE
diplomat

GEORGE WASHINGTON CARVER
botanist

CHARLES WADDELL CHESTNUTT
author

PAUL CUFFE
abolitionist

FREDERICK DOUGLASS
abolitionist editor

CHARLES R. DREW
physician

W. E. B. DUBOIS
educator and author

PAUL LAURENCE DUNBAR
poet

DUKE ELLINGTON
bandleader and composer

RALPH ELLISON
author

ELLA FITZGERALD
singer

MARCUS GARVEY
black-nationalist leader

PRINCE HALL
social reformer

WILLIAM HASTIE
educator and politician

MATTHEW HENSON
explorer

CHESTER HIMES
author

BILLIE HOLIDAY
singer

JOHN HOPE
educator

LENA HORNE
entertainer

LANGSTON HUGHES
poet

JAMES WELDON JOHNSON
author

SCOTT JOPLIN
composer

MARTIN LUTHER KING, JR.
civil rights leader

JOE LOUIS
heavyweight champion

MALCOLM X
militant black leader

THURGOOD MARSHALL
Supreme Court justice

ELIJAH MUHAMMAD
religious leader

JESSE OWENS
champion athlete

GORDON PARKS
photographer

SIDNEY POITIER
actor

ADAM CLAYTON POWELL, JR.
political leader

A. PHILIP RANDOLPH
labor leader

PAUL ROBESON
singer and actor

JACKIE ROBINSON
baseball great

JOHN RUSSWURM
publisher

SOJOURNER TRUTH
antislavery activist

HARRIET TUBMAN
antislavery activist

NAT TURNER
slave revolt leader

DENMARK VESEY
slave revolt leader

MADAME C. J. WALKER
entrepreneur

BOOKER T. WASHINGTON
educator

WALTER WHITE
political activist

RICHARD WRIGHT
author

ON ACHIEVEMENT

Coretta Scott King

Before You Begin this book, I hope you will ask yourself what the word *excellence* means to you. I think that it's a question we should all ask and keep asking as we grow older and change. Because the truest answer to it should never change. When you think of excellence, perhaps you think of success at work; or of becoming wealthy; or meeting the right person, getting married, and having a good family life.

Those important goals are worth striving for, but there is a better way to look at excellence. As Martin Luther King, Jr., said in one of his last sermons, "I want you to be first in love. I want you to be first in moral excellence. I want you to be first in generosity. If you want to be important, wonderful. If you want to be great, wonderful. But recognize that he who is greatest among you shall be your servant."

My husband, Martin Luther King, Jr., knew that the true meaning of achievement is service. When I met him, in 1952, he was already ordained as a Baptist preacher and was working toward a doctoral degree at Boston University. I was studying at the New England Conservatory and dreamed of accomplishments in music. We married a year later, and after I graduated the following year we moved to Montgomery, Alabama. We didn't know it then, but our notions of achievement were about to undergo a dramatic change.

You may have read or heard about what happened next. What began with the boycott of a local bus line grew into a national movement, and by the time he was assassinated in 1968 my husband had fashioned a black movement powerful enough to shatter forever the practice of racial segregation. What you may not have read about is where he got his method for resisting injustice without compromising his religious beliefs.

He adopted the strategy of nonviolence from a man of a different race, who lived in a distant country, and even practiced a different religion. The man was Mahatma Gandhi, the great leader of India, who devoted his life to serving humanity in the spirit of love and nonviolence. It was in these principles that Martin discovered his method for social reform. More than anything else, those two principles were the key to his achievements.

This book is about black Americans who served society through the excellence of their achievements. It forms a part of the rich history of black men and women in America—a history of stunning accomplishments in every field of human endeavor, from literature and art to science, industry, education, diplomacy, athletics, jurisprudence, even polar exploration.

Not all of the people in this history had the same ideals, but I think you will find something that all of them have in common. Like Martin Luther King, Jr., they all decided to become "drum majors" and serve humanity. In that principle—whether it was expressed in books, inventions, or song—they found something outside themselves to use as a goal and a guide. Something that showed them a way to serve others, instead of living only for themselves.

Reading the stories of these courageous men and women not only helps us discover the principles that we will use to guide our own lives but also teaches us about our black heritage and about America itself. It is crucial for us to know the heroes and heroines of our history and to realize that the price we paid in our struggle for equality in America was dear. But we must also understand that we have gotten as far as we have partly because America's democratic system and ideals made it possible.

We are still struggling with racism and prejudice. But the great men and women in this series are a tribute to the spirit of our democratic ideals and the system in which they have flourished. And that makes their stories special and worth knowing. ◆

JAMES
BALDWIN

"WITNESS TO THE TRUTH"

O N THE NIGHT of May 11, 1963, after weeks of continuous racial unrest, the sound of shattering glass ripped through Birmingham, Alabama. Moments later, smoke enveloped Room 30 of the A. G. Gaston Motel. The building, it soon became apparent, had been firebombed.

For more than a month, the Reverend Martin Luther King, Jr., had been using the room as his headquarters. A prominent civil rights leader from Atlanta, Georgia, he had come to Birmingham to direct a citywide campaign against racial segregation. At the time of the attack, however, he was not in his room. He had returned to his home in Atlanta for the weekend.

Nevertheless, the intent of the bombing had been to take his life, and it was the second explosion to occur in Birmingham on that very night. An hour earlier, the home of King's brother, the Reverend A. D. King, had also been struck by segregationists in support of the whites who controlled the city's political power. Fortunately, no one had been killed in either attack. Yet the two blasts had shattered all

Birmingham, Alabama, was among the most racially segregated cities in the South when it was hit by a wave of black violence that left nine city blocks in flames on the night of May 11, 1963. Baldwin, as part of his self-proclaimed mission to "bear witness to the truth," immediately contacted U.S. attorney general Robert Kennedy, the nation's chief legal counsel, to discuss the crisis, which he considered "a matter of national life or death."

In The Fire Next Time, *a set of essays published in 1963, Baldwin launched a searing attack on the state of American race relations. "Color," he wrote, "is not a human or a personal reality; it is a political reality . . . a distinction so hard to make that the West has not been able to make it yet."*

hopes for peace between the city's black and white communities.

In the aftermath of the bombings, Birmingham's black community unleashed its pent-up fury in a night of fire and bloodshed. Thousands of angry blacks roamed the city streets, smashing windows and torching blocks of houses. Pitched battles between rioters and the Birmingham police, who had been beating and arresting black civil rights marchers for weeks, erupted in many sections of the city.

The violence subsided by the morning of May 12, and the first units of 3,000 federal troops sent by President John F. Kennedy began to arrive in Birmingham. Order was soon restored, but order was not the same as peace. The president and his brother, U.S. attorney general Robert F. Kennedy, knew that no amount of troops could bring about a lasting alliance in the city. That would occur only after the blacks' demands for freedom and equality were addressed.

As the Kennedys and their advisers were groping for a way to calm the racial hostilities on the day after the Birmingham riot, the attorney general received a telegram from James Baldwin, one of the most celebrated black authors and lecturers in the United States. The 38-year-old Baldwin said in his message:

> THIS CRISIS IS NEITHER REGIONAL NOR RACIAL. IT IS A MATTER OF THE NATIONAL LIFE OR DEATH. NO TRUCE CAN BE BINDING UNTIL THE AMERICAN PEOPLE AND OUR REPRESENTATIVES ARE ABLE TO ACCEPT THE SIMPLE FACT THAT THE NEGRO IS A MAN.

Baldwin's message outlined with stark simplicity the dangerous state of America's racial problems. At that moment, few people were better qualified to comment on the crisis than Baldwin, who had devoted his life to writing about the powerful sense of alienation that blacks and other minority groups felt in American society. In his book *The Fire Next Time*, which was published earlier in the year, he accused his white countrymen of destroying the lives of black citizens in "the fire of human cruelty." He warned that catastrophe awaited America unless it made a major effort to rid itself of racial hatred.

Baldwin's warning came at a time when racial tensions threatened to engulf the United States in a civil war. A century after the Emancipation Proclamation had ended slavery, blacks were still being subjected to a wide variety of restrictions on their civil liberties. Throughout the South, segregationist regulations known as Jim Crow laws stripped blacks of their voting rights and prevented them from sharing public rest rooms, drinking fountains, schools, and lunch counters with whites. Southern white supremacist groups, such as the Ku Klux Klan, waged terror attacks against blacks, torturing and lynching those who tried to bring about change. Discrimination against blacks outside the South was only slightly less pronounced, with poverty and violence striking at the heart of black communities throughout the country.

Black civil rights marchers are hosed down by the Birmingham fire department in 1963. All black Americans, Baldwin wrote in The Fire Next Time, "must now share the fate of a nation that has never accepted them, to which they were brought in chains. Well, if this is so, one has no choice but to do all in one's power to change that fate, and at no matter what risk."

In response, black activists in the South organized a powerful civil rights movement that was attacking racism at its roots. Baldwin, a northern writer who was noted for his ability to convey the hopes and frustrations of all black Americans, closely observed the growth of the protest movement in the South. He traveled to Atlanta and heard Martin Luther King preach about the need for a campaign of nonviolent resistance to segregation. He accompanied the political activists James Meredith and Medgar Evers as they attempted to organize black community groups in Mississippi.

Baldwin often drew on the scenes he witnessed during his travels across the country and incorporated them into his many novels, essays, and plays. In *The Fire Next Time* and other works, he liked to use his personal encounters to focus attention on the gaping division between blacks and whites. He generally did so while employing a sharp, acerbic writing style that sliced directly into the racial issues that many Americans wished to ignore.

Baldwin's efforts did not go unnoticed. He became not only a best-selling author but a leading black spokesman as well, with books such as *The Fire Next Time* receiving praise from *Newsweek* magazine as a "final plea . . . to end the racial nightmare." In fact, his fame as a commentator on race relations became

Participants in the Children's Crusade, a demonstration against segregation that was held in Birmingham in early May 1963, are marched off to jail by the local police. The harsh treatment of these youthful activists sparked widespread public outrage.

so great that during the third week in May 1963 he was featured on the cover of another of the country's largest-circulating publications, *Time* magazine.

On May 22, as front-page stories and grim photographs of the racial unrest in Alabama were displayed next to Baldwin's picture at the newsstands, a desperate Robert F. Kennedy asked the writer to come to the nation's capital to discuss ways of dealing with the crisis in Birmingham. They met on the following day to talk about the need for the U.S. government to make the campaign for civil rights, as Baldwin said, a "moral issue." Neither this meeting nor a subsequent one left Baldwin encouraged, however. The U.S. government seemed unwilling to provide national leadership in the civil rights campaign.

But the Kennedy administration, much to Baldwin's surprise, did not abandon the civil rights cause. In a public address on June 12, President Kennedy declared that segregation was morally wrong and promised that the federal government would take stronger measures to end racial discrimination. Baldwin's joy at the president's announcement was shattered on the following day, when he heard the news that civil rights activist Medgar Evers had been gunned down in front of his home in Jackson, Mississippi. Yet another courageous freedom fighter had been murdered by the opponents of equal rights, and again the country teetered on the brink of racial warfare.

America and the civil rights movement were, it seemed, at a crossroads. With rampant racial violence threatening to explode into a major conflagration, many blacks were asking, as Baldwin asked in *The Fire Next Time*, "Do I really want to be integrated into a burning house?" Baldwin knew that the answer to this question lay in the days and weeks that were to follow. Moreover, he hoped that his writings would provide a much clearer vision of how America could avoid the road to ruin and march instead along a path to greater human understanding. ✥

Racial disturbances in Birmingham and other cities deeply troubled President John Kennedy (right), shown here conferring with his brother, U.S. attorney general Robert Kennedy. The president announced in June 1963, "The time has come for this nation to fulfill its promise," and he called on all Americans to repudiate segregation.

2

A SON
OF HARLEM

JAMES ARTHUR BALDWIN was born in New York City on August 2, 1924. Until he reached his late teens, he lived in Harlem, the black ghetto at the northern tip of Manhattan in New York City. He later discussed the powerful influence that the ghetto exerted in shaping his character (in a collection of essays entitled *Notes of a Native Son*): "I was born in Harlem. I was raised in Harlem and, indeed, as long as I live I'll never be able to leave Harlem."

Although Harlem is geographically connected to the rest of New York City, at the time of James's birth it might as well have been on an entirely different continent. The district was racially segregated and culturally distinct from the rest of Manhattan and unfamiliar to all but a few whites. In the early 1920s, the blacks who moved to Harlem from the South, the West Indies, and the midtown slums of New York looked upon Harlem as an enclave of opportunity. As the years passed, however, the black district became a place of both extreme pride and extreme desperation, because only a few of the people who moved to its crowded and impoverished slum areas ever realized their dream of earning a good living and buying a house in Sugar Hill, the well-to-do black section of Harlem.

Baldwin was raised in New York City, in the black district known as Harlem. He lived at the upper end of Park Avenue, which was split by a railroad line running out of Grand Central Station that connected midtown Manhattan to all points north.

During the 1920s and 1930s, revelers flocked to Harlem to hear the exciting jazz bands led by Duke Ellington, Fletcher Henderson, and other luminaries. The Cotton Club was among the area's most celebrated night spots.

Yet Harlem at the time of James's birth still held a special allure to black Americans. This was largely because of the artistic and intellectual revolution that was launched in the early 1920s and came to be known as the Harlem Renaissance. Black life and culture were celebrated in novels, poems, and essays by such Harlem-based writers as Langston Hughes, Claude McKay, and Zora Neale Hurston.

An exciting blend of black musical styles, called jazz, also began to sweep the district during the 1920s. Small's Paradise, the Cotton Club, and other night spots in Harlem presented song-and-dance routines that featured hot new sounds and exciting rhythms. Bandleader Duke Ellington and pianist Thomas "Fats" Waller were among the noted entertainers who drew people from all over the city to these clubs. Many whites, from college students to celebrities, made the trek uptown to savor the music and the nightlife in the "great playground," as Harlem was sometimes known.

Nevertheless, the glitter of Harlem's lively cabarets—many of which catered to whites-only audiences—did not hide from view the area's less glamorous side. The majority of the people who lived in the crowded tenement buildings near the Cotton Club were poor and uneducated. Most families had to wage an exhausting struggle against poverty, disease, and unemployment to pay the rent and put food on the table. It was in such a family that James grew up.

The Baldwin family history is a tangled web that would leave many emotional scars on James. A slightly built boy with a wide mouth and large eyes, he was the only child of Emma Berdis Jones and her first husband, a man whom James never knew. He grew up believing that his mother's second husband, David Baldwin, was his father, and it was not until he was in his teens that he discovered that David was actually his stepfather.

James took few happy memories away from his poverty-stricken childhood, which he later described in the essays that compose *Notes of a Native Son*. He grew up in a large family, he said, because of his mother's "exasperating and mysterious habit of having babies." Except for his stepbrother Samuel (who was the product of David Baldwin's first marriage), James was the eldest child. His other siblings were George, Barbara, Wilmer, David, Gloria, Ruth, Elizabeth, and Paula Maria.

James was close to his mother, a stern but kind woman who hailed from Maryland and worked as a maid. She often asked him to look after his younger brothers and sisters while she was out of the apartment. This meant pushing the infants in a stroller, protecting them from the rats that scurried across the apartment floor, and tucking them into bed at night. Sometimes when Emma returned home, she found James holding a book with one hand and a baby with the other.

James was less inclined to perform favors for his stepfather, who had been a Baptist preacher in New Orleans. Domineering and short-tempered, David Baldwin worked during the week at a bottling plant, where he barely earned enough money to feed his large family, and preached in a local church on week-

Harlem youths in 1927. Baldwin, in his essay "The Harlem Ghetto," said that his neighborhood "has changed very little in my parents' lifetime or in mine. Now as then the buildings are old and in desperate need of repair, the streets are crowded and dirty, there are too many human beings per square block."

ends. He had a fierce hatred for whites, whom he blamed in his sermons for all the evil in the world. He was also a rigid disciplinarian who forbade his children from enjoying such diversions as playing marbles, going to the movies, and listening to jazz on the radio. James thought twice before disobeying his stepfather's orders, for he knew that if he were caught, he would be severely punished.

In addition to being afraid of his stepfather, James became convinced that David found him ugly and worthless. He tried desperately to earn his stepfather's approval and love, but all his efforts were rebuffed. The constant rejection eventually sparked a flame of rebellion in James. "The one thing my father did do for me," he wrote later, "was that he taught me how to fight. I had to know how to fight because I fought him so hard." In time, James would search for the causes of his stepfather's harsh outlook on the world and, as he began to understand the corrosive effect that racism had on him, would feel sympathy for the proud and unbending minister.

The turbulence in the Baldwin household helped propel James into the world of books, where he found refuge from his stepfather's ferocious temper. He was not content just to read books; he decided at an early age that he wanted to write them. "I began plotting novels," he said, "about the time I learned to read." By the time he was nine, he had even completed a short play.

David Baldwin's low opinion of his stepson was not shared by the teachers at Public School 24 in Harlem, which James began attending when he was 6 years old. His teachers thought he was bright and talented, and they encouraged his interest in literature and writing. James was especially pleased that he was well regarded by school principal Gertrude Ayer, who was the only black to hold such a position in the entire city school system. She urged the shy, skinny boy to set his sights high, telling him that a writer's career was within his reach.

One teacher who made a lasting impression on James was the school's drama instructor, a young white woman named Orilla Miller. She was impressed with the budding writer and staged his first play in her classroom. She tried to encourage him to continue playwriting by taking him to his first theater performance. Although this was one of the activities that James's stepfather had forbidden to his children, the drama instructor was able to overcome David's objections, and James was permitted to go.

Over the next several years, Miller took more than a passing interest in the Baldwin family. Most notably, she gave them some much-needed financial assistance when David was laid off from work. Because the only whites with whom the Baldwins had had any previous acquaintance were officious welfare workers and demanding bill collectors, Miller's kindness was somewhat puzzling. Her actions were, James said later, "my first key, my first clue that white people were human."

After school, when James was not doing chores or minding the other children, he played in the garbage-strewn lots near his home on upper Park Avenue. There, beside the railroad tracks, he watched the trains speed by on their way to and from the suburbs. Sometimes he walked to Central Park, the large swath of woods and grass in the middle of Manhattan. From the top of his favorite hill, he was able to survey Harlem and the white neighborhoods that beckoned from lower Manhattan.

When James was 10 years old, an encounter with 2 white policemen gave him his first bitter taste of racial violence. The officers spotted him playing by himself in an empty lot and decided to harass him. They taunted him with racial slurs, then beat him and left him flat on his back. "I can conceive of no

One of the leading black educators in New York City, Gertrude Ayer was the principal of Harlem's Public School 24, which Baldwin began attending when he was six years old. She helped the youngster realize that his horizons need not be limited by his poverty.

Negro native to this country," he wrote in "The Harlem Ghetto," "who has not, by the age of puberty, been irreparably scarred by the conditions of his life."

The world of books became James's chief refuge. He made numerous trips each week to local libraries, and his appetite for new reading material soon became so ravenous that he consumed books, he said, as if they were "some kind of weird food." One of his favorite books was *A Tale of Two Cities*, Charles Dickens's romantic saga about the French Revolution. Another book he read over and over was Harriet Beecher Stowe's antislavery novel *Uncle Tom's Cabin*. This book, which became an international best-seller shortly after it was published in 1852, was written to

The faculty and students at Frederick Douglass Junior High in Harlem were quick to recognize Baldwin's talents as a writer. "I always wrote the school plays and all that jazz," he said.

protest the brutal treatment of black slaves by southern slave owners. It was the first adult book James ever read, and it made him realize that white society viewed blacks with contempt.

After graduating from elementary school, James attended Frederick Douglass Junior High School in Harlem. At this school, which was named after the 19th-century antislavery leader and abolitionist editor, he continued to excel in his classwork, and his writing ability won high praise from his teachers. The only problems he experienced were with the other students. They taunted him about his looks and his lack of athletic ability: James's large, bulbous eyes (which earned him the nickname "Popeyes") and broad, toothy grin were a natural target for classroom wiseacres. "He was small and funny-looking," one classmate recalled, "and the kids picked on him cruelly."

Again, James turned to writing as a refuge. "Writing was my great consolation," he said. "I could be as grotesque as a dwarf, and that wouldn't matter."

James's development as a writer was greatly assisted by the faculty at Frederick Douglass Junior High. The school had an excellent reputation, and the teachers set top standards for their students. Among the most notable faculty members was Countee Cullen, a renowned poet of the Harlem Renaissance.

James studied French under the charismatic Cullen, who also served as faculty adviser to the school's literary club. Cullen stoked the students' ambition by introducing them to the works of Langston Hughes, Arna Bontemps, and other prominent black writers. A well-traveled man, he also entertained the pupils with stories about Paris and other places far beyond the confines of Harlem. Cullen's reminiscences ultimately sparked James's desire to seek adventure in foreign lands.

Countee Cullen was one of the most celebrated poets of the Harlem Renaissance. A French teacher and literary club adviser at Frederick Douglass Junior High, he inspired Baldwin with stories of his travels to France and other countries.

Baldwin's first excursion out of Harlem was to midtown Manhattan, where the main building of the New York Public Library was located. Thereafter, he went to the library regularly to research articles for the Douglass Pilot, *his school newspaper.*

Another teacher at Frederick Douglass whom James admired was Herman Porter, a mathematics instructor who also served as faculty adviser to the school newspaper, the *Douglass Pilot.* Porter took the promising young writer under his wing, providing helpful critical advice on the short stories, essays, reviews, and editorials that James submitted to the *Pilot.* Guided by Porter, James began to write well-crafted and lively articles about Harlem's history, its street derelicts, and other subjects that piqued his interest.

In an effort to broaden James's resources as a writer, Porter decided to take him to the main branch of the New York Public Library, an imposing, mammoth structure at Fifth Avenue and 42nd Street in the heart of midtown Manhattan. This was an unexplored part of the city for James. Like most Harlem residents, he considered the midtown area to be "white" territory, a place of unknown dangers. He was so nervous the first time he accompanied Porter to the library that as they made their way downtown he vomited on the bus. Despite this incident, the trip proved to be a rewarding experience for James, who was astounded by the wealth of books available at the library, and he began to go there often.

In 1937, during his final year at Frederick Douglass, James became editor in chief of the *Pilot.* In a farewell editorial he composed for the graduation issue of the newspaper, he wrote about his desire to become a playwright. He wanted, he said, "to be numbered among the great artists of my race." Full of confidence at the age of 14, he had little inkling of the roadblocks that lay ahead of him on the way out of Harlem.

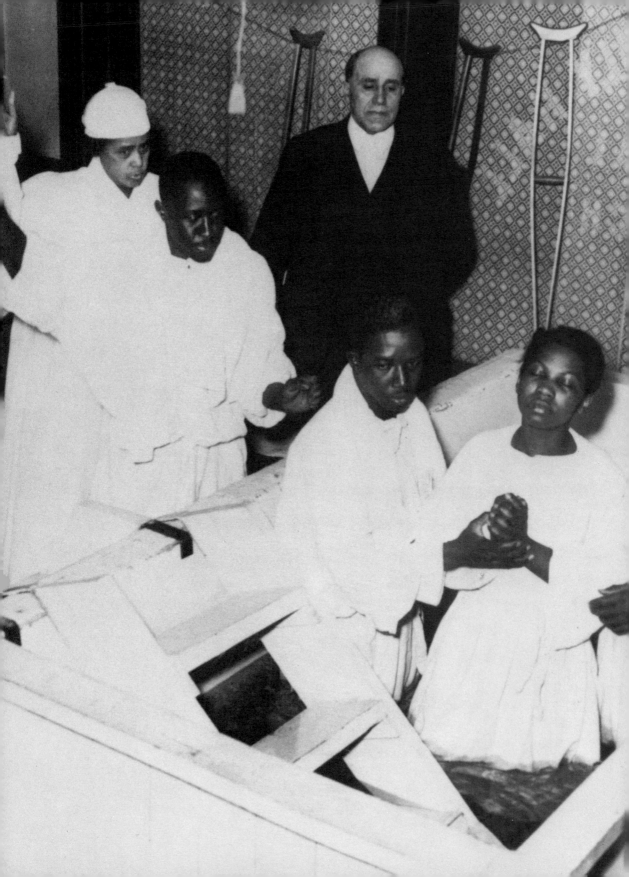

3
DOWN FROM
THE MOUNTAINTOP

❦

JAMES ENTERED A whole new world in the autumn of 1938, when he enrolled at De Witt Clinton High School. Located in the Bronx, the New York City borough just north of Harlem, the school stood on vast, tree-lined grounds. It had an ornate main building that was far different from the stark structures of other schools he had attended. Moreover, the high school had an all-male, mainly white student body.

Most of James's junior high school classmates had chosen either to attend one of the city's vocational training programs or to drop out of school and look for work. As a result, the shy 14-year-old saw few familiar faces on his first day at De Witt Clinton and had some difficulty adjusting to his new classmates, the majority of whom came from a background that was entirely different from his own. Each night, he returned home by subway to the grim surroundings of his slum neighborhood while his classmates headed for their comfortable middle-class homes.

James's inability to fit in with the other students was also due in part to his relatively sheltered youth. He had been raised by his stepfather to follow a strict moral code and had been ordered to ignore the host of temptations that awaited him outside their apartment: Sex, drugs, and gambling were a few of the forbidden activities that beckoned from the Harlem streets. The conflict between his adolescent yearnings and his stepfather's warnings made him, he said,

The streets near Baldwin's Harlem apartment were lined with small storefront churches that often featured emotionally charged baptism ceremonies like the one shown here. Baldwin became a fiery-tongued preacher at the age of 14, after undergoing a soul-wrenching religious experience.

27

"afraid of the evil within me and afraid of the evil without."

Seeking a refuge from his doubts about himself, James turned to religion, which played a vital part in the life of most Harlemites. Hundreds of churches—from the grand Abyssinian Baptist Church headed by the Reverend Adam Clayton Powell, Jr., to the smallest basement or storefront meeting place—dotted the streets of the district. Each of these churches offered its congregation a sense of community, a place to socialize, and a temporary escape from the worries of poverty. Some religious groups, such as the Peace Mission movement directed by the colorful and controversial Father Divine, even provided low-cost food, housing, and health care to the public.

The Harlem church congregations were presided over by ministers, spiritualists, and self-appointed prophets. One breed of especially expressive preachers was known as the Holy Rollers because of their booming voices and wild gestures and movements. They bombarded their audiences with stories about the torments of hell that awaited the sinful and the joys of heaven in store for the pious, and they also lashed out at the sins of Babylon, the name they gave to white society. Occasionally, members of a congregation became so moved by their preacher's inspired performances that they succumbed to trances, fainting spells, and visions. These intense religious experiences, or "conversions," led members to profess a new or stronger commitment to their faith.

On Sunday mornings throughout his youth, James went to the small churches where his stepfather preached. By the time he was 14, he began to accompany a friend, Art Moore, to a church where a dynamic minister named Mother Horn preached to a packed house. Soon afterward, James started attending the Fireside Pentecostal Assembly, a storefront church presided over by the Reverend Theophilus Sobers. One night, while the troubled young man was watching the faithful clap hands and sing hymns, he suddenly fell on the floor and was temporarily blinded by a vision of a being he believed to be God. This penetrating religious experience freed him from his doubts about his morality, and it also sparked in him a desire to be a minister.

The Reverend Sobers was delighted when he learned of James's wish to preach, and the minister arranged for him to stand at the pulpit once a week on various nights, sometimes on Sunday. "He was a very hot speaker," said his friend Art Moore. Impassioned and eloquent, James brought his listeners to peaks of religious fervor. They punctuated the young Holy Roller's sermons with shouts of "Hallelujah!" and "Praise the Lord!" (He later dramatized his experiences as a youthful preacher in his first novel, *Go Tell It on the Mountain*.)

James's popularity as a preacher made his relationship with his stepfather even more prickly. David had driven away most of the members of his congregations with his caustic, hate-filled sermons, and he was jealous of his stepson's success. The distance that separated the young preacher from his stepfather widened even more after James overheard an argument between his parents in which it was revealed that David was not his real father. The truth, which James had suspected for years, made him feel even less comfortable at home than ever before.

Gradually, James began to make friends with a group of students who shared his passion for literature. He maintained a kind of double life for a while, keeping his role as a preacher hidden from his classmates and keeping his associations with white students a secret at home and in church. He knew that his stepfather and the Fireside Pentecostal Assembly members would be angered to learn that he had a

number of close friends who were white. What would be even worse in the eyes of his stepfather was that the majority of his friends were Jewish. David considered Jews to be among the worst of the sinners he consigned to the depths of hell.

James continued to associate with his white friends even after his family found out about them. His best friends at De Witt Clinton were Emile Capouya, who later became a well-known writer, editor, and teacher, and Richard Avedon, who later became one of the most successful photographers in the world. The three were united by their interests in fine literature and intellectual films, and they liked to discuss the latest ideas that were emerging from Greenwich Village, the city's leading center of the arts.

When Baldwin was 14, he began attending De Witt Clinton High School (in the background at left), a mainly white school in the Bronx. He was an editor of the school's literary magazine and spent much of his time with a group of friends who shared his interest in the arts.

Baldwin, Capouya, and Avedon were all members of the editorial board of the school's literary and arts magazine, the *Magpie*. They often cut their afternoon gym classes and sneaked off to meet in a high tower at school that served as the *Magpie*'s office. James said, "The first home I found outside of my own home was that tower." He greatly enjoyed preparing the *Magpie* for publication, and the stories, poems, essays, and book and film reviews he contributed to the magazine helped him develop his talent for evoking the details of everyday life and turning them into high drama.

The more time James put into his writing, the less he put into his schoolwork. Consequently, his grades fell far below what they had been in junior

A Harlem church congregation engages in a hymn-singing session. Baldwin's religious faith gradually eroded during his three years as a "Holy Roller" preacher. "Being in the pulpit was like being in the theater," he said. "I was behind the scenes and knew how the illusion was worked."

high school. In his first year at De Witt Clinton, the former star student scraped by with a grade average of 63, failing both geometry and Spanish.

James's almost total immersion in writing and intellectual debates with his friends affected not only his grades but also his religious faith. When he openly discussed his religious beliefs with his school friends, he found that they were skeptical of his preaching activities. Their views were reinforced by many of his favorite authors, especially Fyodor Dostoyevsky, a Russian author who saw all the pomp and miracles lauded by the church as a sham.

The activities of some of Harlem's less scrupulous ministers were another factor that weakened James's devotion to the church. He was disturbed to see some of his fellow preachers acquiring fancy houses and driving Cadillacs while their parishioners squeezed out their last dimes and nickels for the churches' offering plates.

By the time James reached the end of high school, his religious faith had nearly vanished. Some of the short stories he wrote for the *Magpie* during his final semesters even took on a distinctly antireligious tone. His drift from grace did not escape the notice of his stepfather, who surprised the 17 year old one day by saying to him, "You'd rather write than preach, wouldn't you?"

James had come to the same conclusion. "The end of my youth," he wrote in the introduction to *Nobody Knows My Name*, "was signaled by the reluctant realization that I had, indeed, become a writer; so far so good; now I would have to go the distance." Indeed, breaking with the church after three years of preaching remained an agonizing experience for him. Ultimately, he decided to clear his conscience for good and told the Reverend Sobers that he was leaving the ministry.

James's last year in high school was a tumultuous one for both himself and the world at large. In December 1941, the Japanese launched a surprise attack on the U.S. naval base at Pearl Harbor. The United States immediately declared war on Japan and its allies, Italy and Germany, thus entering World War II. At the same time, David's health began to deteriorate rapidly from tuberculosis, forcing him to stop working. The economic fortunes of the already poverty-stricken Baldwin family spiraled downward and hit rock bottom.

Despite his family's hardship, James managed to make it through his senior year of high school. Most of his classmates graduated from De Witt Clinton in June 1942, and he received his diploma six months later, after he completed some makeup work. He hoped that his achievement of finishing school would serve as an example to his brothers and sisters. None of them went on to graduate from high school, however. In his family, as well as outside it, James stood alone.

Winnette's DRESSES
COLORED STORE
Colored Store
COLORED STORE
COLORED STORE
COLORED STORE
COLORED STORE

4

THE WORLD
OF WORDS

B Y THE TIME James Baldwin graduated from high school in 1942, he had already decided to become a professional writer. Yet he was expected to help support his hard-pressed family, and the only work that was readily available involved manual labor. Consequently, he worked as a porter, handyman, and elevator operator during the day. He started writing a novel during his spare hours at night in his family's crowded home.

Little time had passed before Baldwin resolved to move away from his family's Harlem apartment. When Emile Capouya, who was employed at a military defense plant in New Jersey, told him during the summertime that plenty of jobs were available at the factory, he decided to make the short journey west. There the two teenagers worked together on a crew that constructed an army supply depot. Baldwin was assigned to a job on the railroad, then on the cinder gang, and finally at the warehouse, where he loaded and unloaded boxcars.

The hours at the defense plant were long, but the pay was good. Capouya, who came from a white middle-class family, found the hard work a "stimulating new experience." Baldwin, who was used to manual

The Harlem community's predominantly white-owned business district was gutted in August 1943, when a massive race riot erupted in the streets. Some black businessmen placed Colored Store signs in their windows in the hope that looters would spare their property.

labor, did not share his friend's excitement at shoveling coal. Instead, he duly noted the racial bigotry he was forced to encounter.

New York City was by no means a paradise for blacks. But Baldwin's hometown did not feature the overt bigotry that pervaded the South and some parts of the North, including the area around the defense plant where he worked. Local statutes in New Jersey enforced the same kind of Jim Crow laws that were practiced in the South. These laws prohibited blacks from entering public washrooms, theaters, restaurants, and stores visited by whites.

In Harlem, blacks were rarely barred from patronizing businesses in their own neighborhood, and Baldwin's insistence on ignoring segregation practices in New Jersey soon got him into trouble. His difficulties began when he tried to eat at the same restaurants where his white coworkers dined. Time after time, the 18 year old was told by the waiters that blacks were not served there. Baldwin was deeply upset by these bans, and he started to let out his frustrations at work, where he refused to act subserviently to whites.

Baldwin was fired for his defiance, but he was rehired after some white friends interceded on his behalf. Then he was fired and rehired once more. When he was fired for a third time, in July 1943, he did not get his job back.

There was nothing for Baldwin to do but return to Harlem. Before making the trip, however, he decided to enjoy one last night out with a friend from work. They went to a segregated eating place for whites instead of a restaurant that welcomed blacks.

As soon as Baldwin entered the establishment he heard those hated words: "We don't serve Negroes here." This time his anger boiled over, and he hurled a mug at the waitress who refused to serve him. The object missed its target and shattered a mirror on the wall. The sound of the crash brought Baldwin back to his senses. He kicked free of a man who had grasped hold of him and managed to escape before the police arrived.

The incident marked the first and last time Baldwin ever resorted to violence. His fit of blinding rage had given him the sense that his life was in danger "not from anything other people might do," he said, "but from the hatred I carried in my own heart." He resolved to find a way other than violence to strike back at bigotry and racism.

Yet Baldwin could not escape the violence. When he returned to Harlem at the end of July 1943, he

The center of Harlem's business district on the morning after the August 1943 riot. "Harlem had needed something to smash," Baldwin said in describing the furious mood that existed throughout the ghetto in the days before the riot. "To smash something is the ghetto's chronic need."

found himself in the middle of a highly charged community on the verge of exploding. Word had spread throughout the district that most northern blacks, having enlisted in the United States Army to fight in World War II, were being treated badly at training camps in the South. It was yet another outrage that black Americans could add to their long list of grievances.

On August 1, one day before Baldwin's 19th birthday, a massive riot erupted in New York's black ghetto. Reports that a white policeman had killed a black serviceman in a Harlem hotel initiated the night of rage and violence. Mobs roamed through the streets, looting and burning stores and battling with police and national guardsmen who tried to restore order. During the rioting, five blacks were shot to death, and many more were injured or arrested.

Baldwin's stepfather had died several days earlier, on July 29, and his funeral service was held on the very day that the riot took place. The minister was buried on the following day, August 2, and the funeral procession passed through streets littered with ashes and shards of plate glass. "I truly had not realized that Harlem had so many stores until I saw them all smashed open," Baldwin said later.

The entire scene prompted the 19 year old to admit it was time for him to leave Harlem. The district was destined to become an even poorer and angrier place than it had ever been before. He had already seen far too many people end up on welfare rolls, and if he continued to live there, he, too, would be overcome by its squalor and consumed by its hopelessness.

There was only one thing to do. "I *had* to leave Harlem," he said. "I had to jump *then*." And yet he had to remain nearby and help support his family.

Baldwin's solution was to move downtown to Greenwich Village. This part of the city seemed to

In 1943, Baldwin left Harlem and moved to Greenwich Village, where many of New York's artists and writers lived and worked. One of the ways that the local poets made their works publically available was by posting them on a fence.

be perfectly suited for an aspiring young writer. Every night, musicians, poets, writers, and artists from all over the world discussed their art in the Village's many jazz clubs and cafés.

During the day, Baldwin worked at various jobs: He was a waiter, dishwasher, office worker, shipyard hand, and factory worker. At night, in his cheap, $25-per-month apartment, he continued to refine the novel he had begun several years earlier. In between, he squeezed in a few hours of sleep.

Baldwin soon received some encouragement from an unexpected source. In early 1945, a friend arranged for him to meet with the best-selling author Richard Wright, whose *Native Son* was one of the first novels by a black writer to expose the strong undercurrent of black rage in the United States. Published in 1940, Wright's powerful work made him a hero to many blacks, including Baldwin, who was extremely nervous about their impending meeting. When the 20 year old boarded a subway train to Wright's home in Brooklyn on the appointed day, he was, as he later described himself, "shabby, hungry, and scared."

Richard Wright became the most noted black writer in America as soon as his powerful novel Native Son *was published in 1940. Five years later, he read some of Baldwin's early fiction and helped the struggling writer win his first literary award.*

He need not have been. Wright greeted Baldwin warmly and poured a glass of bourbon for each of them while he talked about the vocation of writing. "There was very little he could tell me," Baldwin recalled, "except that being a writer was very difficult, which I'd already begun to suspect." Nevertheless, he was grateful for the encouragement Wright gave him.

When Baldwin returned home, he wasted no time in sending Wright the first section of his novel in progress (which would be published under the title *Go Tell It on the Mountain* in 1953). Wright was so impressed with Baldwin's work that he recommended the budding novelist to the panel of judges for the Eugene F. Saxton Memorial Trust Award, a grant given to a promising young writer. Baldwin was elated when he learned that he had won the literary prize, which confirmed his status as an accomplished writer.

Baldwin worked feverishly at finishing his novel once he won the award. Yet he could not piece the entire work together. The pressure to prove that he was worthy of Wright's recommendation was too much for him to handle. "I got paralyzed," he said. He thought about asking Wright for his advice on how to proceed, but he was too awed by the older author. Eventually, he shelved the work, feeling guilty that he was betraying Wright's confidence in him. Baldwin realized that he still had much to learn about plotting and constructing a novel.

After setting the manuscript aside, Baldwin decided to work at polishing his craft by writing book reviews. His first review appeared in the *Nation*, a prestigious literary and political journal, and gained him a toehold in the publishing world. He then received assignments from the *New Leader*, another current-affairs journal, to review books that dealt with the racial situation in the United States. His tactic of writing reviews worked: It helped him regain his confidence, and he started to write another novel. (He published this work, which was loosely based on a murder that had occurred in New York in 1943, as *Giovanni's Room* in 1956.)

Throughout this period in Greenwich Village, Baldwin supported himself by working as a busboy, dishwasher, and waiter at a nearby restaurant called Calypso. His shift lasted until midnight. Then, after meeting a few friends for drinks, he went home and wrote. Whatever money he had left after paying for his living expenses went to his mother.

Baldwin's reviews for the *Nation* and the *New Leader* soon caught the attention of the editors of *Commentary*, a periodical published by the American Jewish Committee, and they commissioned him to write a major essay on Harlem. Writing the article forced him to deal with a troubling issue: black anti-Semitism. Although he held Jews in high regard, his opinion was not shared by most blacks in Harlem. They resented the fact that Jews owned a large proportion of the local businesses and real estate. In addition, many of the highly religious blacks were like Baldwin's stepfather, who disliked Jews because of their religious beliefs.

Baldwin felt that the hostility blacks felt toward Jews was unfortunate because both groups were victims of widespread prejudice and would be better off as allies in the struggle for social reform. Nevertheless, he was not eager to examine such a sensitive subject. His editor at *Commentary*, an extremely supportive man named Robert Warshow, convinced him that the issue of black anti-Semitism should be examined at length. "We sweated that piece out," Baldwin said, "because I was really afraid of it."

"The Harlem Ghetto" caused a sensation when it appeared in the February 1948 issue of *Commentary*. In writing about black anti-Semitism, Baldwin exposed a raw nerve in race relations. "I remember

FROM THE AMERICAN SCENE

THE HARLEM GHETTO: WINTER 1948

The Vicious Circle of Frustration and Prejudice

JAMES BALDWIN

HARLEM, physically at least, has changed very little in my parents' lifetime or in mine. Now as then the buildings are old and in desperate need of repair, the streets are crowded and dirty, there are too many human beings per square block. Rents are 10 to 58 per cent higher than anywhere else in the city; food, expensive everywhere, is more expensive here and of an inferior quality; and now that the war is over and money is dwindling, clothes are carefully shopped for and seldom bought. Negroes, traditionally the last to be hired and the first to be fired, are finding jobs harder to get, and, while prices are rising implacably, wages are going down. All over Harlem now there is felt the same bitter expectancy with which, in my childhood, we awaited winter: it is coming and it will be hard, there is nothing anyone can do about it.

All of Harlem is pervaded by a sense of congestion, rather like the insistent, maddening, claustrophobic pounding in the skull that comes from trying to breathe in a very small room with all the windows shut. Yet the white man walking through Harlem is not at all likely to find it sinister and no more wretched than any other slum.

Harlem wears to the casual observer a casual face; no one remarks that—considering the history of black men and women and the legends that have sprung up about them, to say nothing of the ever-present policemen, wary on the street corners—the face is, indeed, somewhat excessively casual and may not be as open or as careless as it seems. If an outbreak of more than usual violence occurs, as in 1935 or in 1943, it is met with sorrow and surprise and rage; the social hostility of the rest of the city feeds on this as proof that they were right all along, and the hostility increases; speeches are made, committees are set up, investigations ensue. Steps are taken to right the wrong, without, however, expanding or demolishing the ghetto. The idea is to make it less of a social liability, a process about as helpful as make-up on a leper. Thus, we have the Boys' Club on West 134th Street, the playground at West 131st and Fifth Avenue; and, since Negroes will not be allowed to live in Stuyvesant Town, Metropolitan Life is thoughtfully erecting a housing project in the center of Harlem called Riverton; however, it is not likely that any but the professional class of Negroes—and not all of them—will be able to pay the rent.

MOST of these projects have been stimulated by perpetually embattled Negro leaders and by the Negro press. Concerning Negro leaders, the best that one can say is that they are in an impossible position and that the handful motivated by genuine concern maintain this position with heartbreaking dignity. It is unlikely that anyone ac-

WHENEVER one ponders the progress of the American ideals of freedom and equality in the framework of today's realities, one inevitably thinks of the South—and of Harlem. How is it in Harlem in the winter of 1948? JAMES BALDWIN's description of the Harlem ghetto also touches upon the delicate and perplexing problem of Negro-Jewish relations in this country, an unhappy complex which requires our best in understanding and courage. Mr. Baldwin was born in New York City in 1924.

165

Baldwin published his first major essay, an article about life in New York's black district entitled "The Harlem Ghetto," in Commentary *magazine in February 1948. His scathing criticism of black newspapers and his charge that most blacks were anti-Semitic angered many people in Harlem and in New York's Jewish community.*

meeting no Negro in the years of my growing up, in my family or out of it," he said, "who would really ever trust a Jew, and few did not, indeed, exhibit for them the blackest contempt." He explained that the cause of much of the ill feeling could be traced to the economic hardships faced by blacks. Predictably, his comments won him few friends among either blacks or Jews.

After writing the *Commentary* article, Baldwin contributed poems and essays to *Partisan Review* and other small magazines. In October 1948, he published his first short story in *Commentary*. That story, called "The Previous Condition," revolves around a bitter young man named Peter who struggles with his identity as a black. At one point in the story, he cries out, "I don't want to hate anybody, but now maybe, I can't love anybody either."

Peter's outburst reflected Baldwin's own morale, which had sunk to an all-time low by the fall of 1948. The long hours he had put into working and writing—not to mention drinking with his friends—finally caught up with him. Exhaustion and poverty overcame his youthful optimism and left him on the brink of depression. Moreover, Greenwich Village had lost most of its charm for him; as one of the area's few black residents, he found himself constantly being harassed by policemen and bigoted whites.

A series of disappointments added to Baldwin's low self-esteem. In 1948, he teamed up with photographer Theodore Pelatowski to put together a book on Harlem's storefront churches. The excellence of Baldwin's manuscript helped him win a fellowship from the Julius Rosenwald Foundation, an organization that channeled some of its funds into supporting black artists. However, he was unable to find a publisher for the book.

At the same time, an important relationship in Baldwin's life ended. For two years, he had been living with a woman for whom he had bought an engagement ring. He decided to break off their engagement because he believed he would not be able to support a family.

The final blow came in late 1948, when one of Baldwin's close friends committed suicide. The distraught writer decided to leave New York before he, too, became a victim of despair. He decided to move outside the United States, to a country where the color of his skin would not cause him so much pain. With the money he received from the Rosenwald fellowship, he bought a one-way ticket to France.

On a chilly November day in 1948, Baldwin boarded an airplane bound for Paris. Although he did not speak any French, did not have any job prospects, and had only $40 to his name, he was determined to forge a new life abroad. "I went out of the country and I never intended to come back here," he said. "Ever. *Ever.*" ◖◗

5

AN AMERICAN
WRITER ABROAD

In 1948, Baldwin decided to leave the United States and moved to France. He arrived in Paris, he said, "with a little over forty dollars in my pockets, nothing in the bank, and no grasp whatever of the French language. It developed, shortly, that I had no grasp of the French character either."

WHEN BALDWIN'S PLANE touched the ground in France, his high hopes fell. Paris on November 12, 1948, was cold and foggy, and the foreignness of the city frightened him. Furthermore, the City of Lights, noted for its beauty and culture, was still recovering from the devastating effects of World War II. Household necessities were scarce; heating, plumbing, and electricity were rarely adequate; the telephones worked poorly, if at all. Baldwin's initial excitement upon seeing Paris and its celebrated cafés quickly evaporated when he discovered the spartan living conditions in the city.

Baldwin was in Paris for less than an hour when he settled down at a table in a café, only to find Richard Wright sitting nearby. Wright, who had been living in France for more than two years, asked Baldwin to join him. The two talked for a while. Then Wright guided Baldwin to an inexpensive hotel and took leave of his 24-year-old disciple. This brief encounter turned out to be the only time the two men socialized with one another in Paris.

Baldwin's spirits sank even lower when he saw the shabby condition of his hotel room. But with his pockets nearly empty, he could not do much better. During his initial weeks in Paris, his $40 disappeared quickly. Unable to pay his hotel bill, he sold first his clothes and then his cherished typewriter. As if that was not enough, he soon became seriously ill because of the cold, damp air that seeped into his poorly heated room.

Confined to bed for weeks, Baldwin might not have survived if not for the kindness of his landlady, who nursed him back to health. Despite her help, he ran up huge bills and had to beg for money from virtual strangers so he could buy back his typewriter. Overwhelmed by his troubles, he "went to pieces," he said later.

Baldwin was evicted from one hotel room after another because of his inability to pay his bills, and he soon discovered that the French were hardly more tolerant of blacks than white Americans were. On one occasion, he was falsely accused of stealing bed sheets from a hotel. After being fingerprinted and handcuffed, he was thrown into a small jail cell. Although he was ultimately acquitted of the theft, he remained convinced that he had been accused of the crime because he was black.

Despite these difficulties, Baldwin eventually became accustomed to Paris. He developed an intimate circle of friends, many of them American expatriates like himself, and began enjoying his adopted city. Because there were not many black Americans in Paris, he felt somewhat special.

Baldwin showed his writing to a number of French editors, and before long, they recognized his unique talent for capturing the complex nature of the human spirit in his work. The first essay he completed in Paris, "Everybody's Protest Novel," was published in *Zéro*, one of the city's leading literary magazines, in June 1949. The essay blasted the black stereotypes found in social-protest literature, ranging from Stowe's *Uncle Tom's Cabin* to Wright's *Native Son*, and asserted that black writers must do more than merely exhibit rage; they must analyze the roots of racial oppression.

"I didn't have to prove anything to anybody," Baldwin said of his time in France. *"I could write, I could think, I could feel, I could walk, I could eat, I could breathe."*

Baldwin took what may have been an imprudent step in criticizing Wright's work. The article deeply hurt the older writer and soured their friendship to such an extent that the two men never had much contact with each other again. Baldwin, who later said he was sorry he had attacked *Native Son* so harshly, regretted that he never offered an apology to Wright before he died in 1960.

In addition to writing essays and reviews, Baldwin plunged back into his first novel. When he was away from his typewriter, he often made the rounds of Paris's literary circles. Constantly broke and scrounging for a meal, he did this in part so he could keep his name circulating among people in the publishing industry. Among the American writers he met were James Jones, Philip Roth, Norman Mailer, and William Styron. Baldwin, according to Styron, "told me more about the frustrations and anguish of being a black man in America than I had known until then, or perhaps wanted to know. He told me exactly what it was like to be denied service, to be spat at."

In 1951, Baldwin again ran into problems with the novel and came close to giving up on the book. Then he realized that the book needed to be reconstructed. He spent the next three months rewriting the novel while staying at a friend's house in a Swiss mountain village.

In February 1952, after working on the novel off and on for 10 years, Baldwin finally completed *Go Tell It on the Mountain*. The story, which is about a boy growing up in Harlem, is largely autobiographical. The main character is 14-year-old John Grimes, who has a tormented relationship with both his tyrannical stepfather, the Reverend Gabriel, and the Temple of the Fire Baptized, the church that he would like to see disappear from his life. The novel captures the spirit of Harlem's storefront churches and Holy Roller sermons as it arrestingly examines racism. By

GROSSET'S
UNIVERSAL
LIBRARY

GO TELL IT ON THE
MOUNTAIN
JAMES BALDWIN

UL 95
$1.45
$1.90 IN CANADA

Baldwin's first novel, the largely autobiographical Go Tell It on the Mountain, *received outstanding reviews when it was published in 1953. The story of a boy's attempt to escape from his stepfather's tormenting shadow was widely acclaimed for its vivid imagery and feverish intensity.*

the end of the novel, Grimes learns to conquer his anger at the world by giving himself up to the healing power of love and compassion.

Baldwin later said that *Go Tell It on the Mountain* was "the book I had to write if I was ever going to write anything else. I had to deal with what hurt me most. I had to deal, above all, with my father. . . . Nobody's ever frightened me since."

When Baldwin returned to Paris, he mailed a copy of the manuscript to Helen Straus, a literary agent he had met in New York. She was greatly impressed with *Go Tell It on the Mountain* and took it to Alfred A. Knopf, one of the most distinguished publishing houses in the country. A short time later, she notified Baldwin that Knopf had accepted his book.

Baldwin was stunned. All of his labors had finally paid off. He borrowed money from actor Marlon Brando, a friend from his Greenwich Village days who was also in Paris, so he could buy a ticket to New York City. Baldwin sailed to his hometown in 1952 and was glad to see his family again and meet with his editor at Knopf. But he stayed in the United States just long enough to discover that he felt uncomfortable visiting his old haunts in Harlem and Greenwich Village. "I came back to a kind of limbo," he said. He had been away from New York for four years, and his friends seemed like strangers.

After spending three months in New York, Baldwin fled to Paris, where he awaited the publication of his first book. In May 1953, the triumphant day arrived. He found 10 brand-new copies of the novel awaiting him at the post office. On the dust jacket was emblazoned not only his name but lavish words of critical praise. It was the fulfillment of his greatest hopes.

The reviews of *Go Tell It on the Mountain* confirmed Baldwin's place as the most gifted black writer to appear in print since Richard Wright. Descriptions of the novel ranged from "beautiful, fierce, extraordinary, powerful" to "brutal, objective, and compassionate." *Commentary* magazine called it "the most important novel written about the American Negro," and the noted critic Lionel Trilling wrote that the novel had laid claim "to all the possible fullness of life, to whatever in art and culture was vivacious, beautiful, and interesting." Popular with both black and white audiences, *Go Tell It on the Mountain* was praised for its engrossing portrayal of life in the black ghetto and for its eloquent attack on racism.

Bolstered by his literary success, Baldwin went back to work on his second novel. Once again, he decided to work at his friend's chalet in Switzerland. As had happened during his first visit, he found himself being scrutinized by the Swiss villagers. He was the first black man some of them had ever seen. In fact, several of the townspeople rubbed his hand to see if the color of his skin came off. Others merely stared.

Not one to let uncomfortable experiences slip by unrecorded, Baldwin included his observations about the town in "Stranger in the Village." That essay, which was published in *Notes of a Native Son*, points out that in the United States a black man is never looked on as such an oddity. "One of the things that distinguishes Americans from other people," the author said, "is that no other people has ever been so deeply involved in the lives of black men, or vice versa."

In 1953, Baldwin moved from Paris to Les Quatre Chemins, a quiet village in the south of France. There he worked on *Giovanni's Room*, which was to become his favorite, as well as his most controversial, novel. He broke new ground in this work. Not only were its characters white—a disconcerting fact for those who had typecast Baldwin as a "Negro novelist"— but the two protagonists were homosexual.

Baldwin knew he was going to have trouble finding an American publisher for *Giovanni's Room* because it dealt with the topic of homosexuality. In an era when any mention of sexual activity was taboo, bold descriptions of homosexuality were definitely unprintable. This proved to be the case when he returned to New York in the summer of 1954 with the first chapters of the manuscript in hand. Publisher

Baldwin worked on his second novel, Giovanni's Room, *in the same tiny Swiss village where he had completed his first novel. His stay in this all-white town prompted him to write an essay, "Stranger in the Village," about the sense of isolation he felt there.*

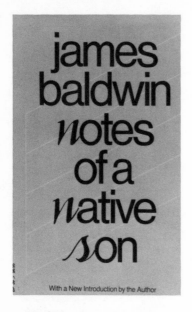

james
baldwin
notes
of a
native
son

With a New Introduction by the Author

Notes of a Native Son, *Baldwin's first book of essays, contained 10 articles he had previously published in magazines. The book, which ends with the assertion "This world is white no longer, and it will never be white again," was widely praised for its incisive look at America's racial problems.*

after publisher rejected it, telling him that his literary career would probably be ruined if the novel were published.

Baldwin was incensed by their response. He called them all cowards and took the book to a small British publisher who was willing to print it. Then a strange thing happened. The editors at Dial Press, a New York–based publishing house, became interested in the manuscript. They offered him a contract for *Giovanni's Room* in addition to his next novel, which he had not even begun. Although Baldwin was annoyed that their publishing agreement called for only a small advance, he accepted it.

Not only did *Giovanni's Room* receive good reviews when it reached the bookstores in 1956, the novel also helped Baldwin win two significant literary awards: a Partisan Review Fellowship and the National Institute of Arts and Letters Award. Apparently, the book's frank discussion of one man's search for personal identity while pursuing a variety of sexual relationships did not offend the public, at least not as much as most New York publishers had feared. Needless to say, Baldwin felt vindicated by the positive response to his book.

The same year that Baldwin finished writing *Giovanni's Room*, he completed his first play, *The Amen Corner*. In writing the drama, he returned to his past as a Harlem preacher. *The Amen Corner* is a morality tale about a minister whose life is ruined by her fanatical devotion to spiritual purity and by her lack of compassion for human failings.

In 1955, the 31-year-old writer published *Notes of a Native Son*, a collection of essays that includes "The Harlem Ghetto," "Stranger in the Village," and "Everybody's Protest Novel." The book records Baldwin's attempt to come to terms with his identity as a black American and offers powerful insights into the nature of the country's racial conflicts.

Notes of a Native Son has since become a landmark work in American literature. It is a collection, according to the poet Langston Hughes, that "should influence for the better all who ponder on the things books say." In one of the essays, "Ruminations Upon the Death of a Father," Baldwin even set down what can be regarded as his personal credo: "One must never, in one's own life accept . . . injustices as commonplace, but must fight them with all one's strength. This fight begins, however, in the heart."

By 1957, Baldwin was in fact beginning to have a change of heart; he started to think about returning to his native country. His life was very comfortable; he had settled on the French island of Corsica in the Mediterranean Sea and had become widely appreciated as a writer. Yet he believed the time had come for him to sink his roots back in American soil. Europe seemed more of a hiding place than a true home for an author who was celebrated for his ability to capture the essence of black America.

"I moved to Europe in 1948," Baldwin said, "because I . . . could not find in my surroundings, in my country, a certain stamina, a certain corroboration that I needed. But there isn't any way ever to leave America." He had managed to free himself of much of the anger he felt toward the United States and was ready to become directly involved in the nation's growing racial struggle. "Once I found myself on the other side of the ocean," he said, "I could see where I came from very clearly."

In July 1957, after nine years spent mainly overseas, Baldwin packed up his belongings and made the long voyage back to New York. "I am the grandson of a slave, and I am a writer," he reasoned. "I must deal with both." ☙

6
LOOKING FOR AMERICA

W HEN BALDWIN RETURNED to the United States in July 1957, he found himself in a country whose racial climate was being dramatically altered by a new, militant civil rights movement. Throughout the South, the Southern Christian Leadership Conference (SCLC), the Congress on Racial Equality (CORE), and other activist organizations were using protest marches, sit-ins, public prayer meetings, and economic boycotts to publicize their demand for an end to Jim Crow oppression. Two months after Baldwin's arrival in America and one month after Congress passed a major civil rights bill that established a civil rights division within the Justice Department, events in Little Rock, Arkansas, shattered forever one of the strongest hallmarks of racial discrimination: school segregation.

The saga began on the September morning that 15-year-old Elizabeth Eckford arrived, notebook in hand, for her first day of classes at Little Rock's all-white Central High School. Unlike most of the school's 2,000 students, Eckford was black. In fact,

In July 1957, Baldwin returned to the United States to take part in the growing civil rights movement. A notable development in the struggle for equal rights took place two months later, when Elizabeth Eckford and eight other black students enrolled in Central High School in Little Rock, Arkansas, as part of a campaign to end racial segregation in the city's public school system.

she was one of only nine black students who had enrolled at the school in the wake of the U.S. Supreme Court's 1954 decision that said it was unconstitutional for public schools to be racially segregated.

The Supreme Court's ruling in *Brown v. the Board of Education of Topeka, Kansas* was a spectacular breakthrough for the American civil rights movement. Beginning with the *Plessy v. Ferguson* case in 1896, the courts had upheld the legality of segregation in schools so long as each segregated public school system provided "separate but equal" education for blacks and whites. Unfortunately, the separate schools rarely turned out to be equal once this ruling was put into effect. The white schools invariably received more funding and had better facilities than the black schools did.

It was not until May 17, 1954, that the Supreme Court struck down its ruling on segregated educational facilities—a historic decision that was greeted with both celebration and cries of outrage. Prominent civil rights activists such as the Reverend Martin Luther King, Jr., hailed the ruling as a "world-shaking decree." Infuriated white segregationists named the day on which the Supreme Court announced its decision "Black Monday."

Clearly, the battle was not yet over. In a show of defiance, the Ku Klux Klan lit fiery crosses in the southern sky to signal the beginning of a concerted effort by segregationists to overturn the Supreme Court's decision. The Arkansas Board of Education, incensed by what it viewed as federal interference in state affairs, went so far as to declare that the court's decree of desegregation was void in that state. Whites in other southern states were equally determined to uphold segregation forever.

In Little Rock, an all-out attempt was made to prevent Elizabeth Eckford and the eight other blacks from attending class at the start of the school year in

A Ku Klux Klansman in the South stands beside a flaming cross, a symbol of the organization's resolve to maintain white supremacy in America. "The South had always frightened me," Baldwin wrote. "How deeply it had frightened me—though I had never seen it—and how soon, was one of the things my dreams revealed to me when I was there."

1957. In flagrant violation of federal law, Arkansas governor Orval Faubus ordered the National Guard to surround Central High and keep the black students from entering. Local officials of the nation's leading antidiscriminatory organization, the National Association for the Advancement of Colored People (NAACP), escorted eight black students past an angry mob to the front of the school. Eckford was the only one to brave the crowds alone.

Confronted by hundreds of armed guardsmen as well as the jeers and taunts of the mob, the "Little Rock Nine" were prevented from entering the building. Three weeks later, after the national troops had left the scene, Eckford and the eight others managed to make their way into the school. They did not remain inside for long, however. Another angry mob created such an ugly disturbance outside Central High that the black students were sent home early.

President Dwight Eisenhower then seized control of the Arkansas National Guard and dispatched an additional force of 1,000 army paratroopers to Little Rock. On September 25, accompanied by federal troops, Eckford and the eight other black students entered their new school after marching past a crowd of hostile whites waving Confederate flags. The changing of the guard at segregated schools across the South had begun in earnest.

When Baldwin had lived in France, he followed the progress of the civil rights movement, including the long campaign led by Martin Luther King to end segregation on the public transportation system in Montgomery, Alabama. While discussing the black activists' sit-ins and protest marches with a Paris taxi driver, Baldwin had suddenly realized that he wanted to go to the South and see the area for himself. He wanted to hear firsthand the stories of the brave black children who were attempting to enroll in previously all-white schools. He also wanted to satisfy his curiosity about the land that had given birth to the blues singer Bessie Smith, the jazz musician Louis Armstrong—and Emma and David Baldwin.

As soon as Baldwin arrived in New York and settled into an apartment, he made plans to visit the South. His journey began in the autumn of 1957, and his first stop was Charlotte, North Carolina. As he approached the town by plane, he realized he was entering a land that had always frightened and mystified him. In his mind, the South was a place of shackles and slavery, lynchings and whippings. Yet it was also the land of his ancestors, and one he could no longer ignore.

After dropping off his bags at a friend's house, Baldwin took a walking tour of Charlotte. It was a beautiful but sleepy town and looked to Baldwin as though it had probably not changed for centuries. Curious about the racial climate there, he asked both whites and blacks for their views on the subject. Whites assured him that the town had no racial troubles. Blacks saw matters differently. For the most part, they felt trapped in a web of poverty and held out little hope that their fortunes would ever improve. As an example, they pointed out that blacks could not obtain licenses to become plumbers or electricians.

When Baldwin brought up the subject of school integration, he was given disappointing news: Only four of the town's black children had even been assigned to white schools. By the time of Baldwin's arrival, only three of the students were still at the schools. The fourth student, Dorothy Counts, had given up after a white mob had pelted her with stones and spat on her. Hearing her story firsthand, Baldwin got a taste of the bitter struggle that lay ahead in the effort to integrate schools in the South.

After spending two weeks in Charlotte, Baldwin moved on to one of the South's largest cities: Atlanta, Georgia. He was not in a pleasant frame of mind as he entered Atlanta. His first thoughts upon seeing the deep red hue of Georgia's clay soil was that the color was a vestige of the blood shed by slaves.

Yet Baldwin could not deny his connection to the land. He saw himself as a son returning to the place of his parents' childhood. He wrote, "The landscape has always been familiar; the speech is archaic, but it rings a bell; and so do the ways of the people."

In the midst of the civil rights movement, Baldwin urged Americans to seek a new national identity based on racial equality. He wrote in Notes of a Native Son, *"The time has come to realize that the interracial drama acted out on the American continent has not only created a new black man, it has created a new white man, too."*

Dorothy Counts is taunted by a white mob as she walks to her first day of classes at an all-white high school in Charlotte, North Carolina, in September 1957. Baldwin interviewed the 15-year-old student shortly after this incident and later wrote about her in a collection of essays, Nobody Knows My Name: More Notes of a Native Son.

During one of his walking tours of Atlanta, Baldwin found to his surprise that the city included a prosperous black community that was somewhat isolated from the rest of the black population. The people in this middle-class community drove their own cars, owned their own homes, and operated their own businesses. Most of these well-to-do blacks supported efforts by Atlanta's white public officials to keep racial unrest to a minimum. They believed such tensions were "bad for business." Nevertheless, the school integration issue upset the city's fragile peace.

While in Atlanta, Baldwin listened to a 15 year old discuss his experiences as the only black student at his high school. (In his book *Nobody Knows My Name: More Notes of a Native Son*, Baldwin refuses to reveal the teenager's name; he calls him "G.") On his third day of classes, the teenager was confronted by a line of hostile white students at the school entrance. Taunted with vicious racial slurs, he was able to make his way into the building only after the principal came to his rescue. "I wonder," the boy's mother said to Baldwin, "what makes white folks so mean."

To help answer some of his own questions, Baldwin arranged to meet with Martin Luther King. The pastor of a Baptist church in Montgomery, Alabama, King had recently emerged as the chief spokesman and spiritual leader of the southern civil rights movement. He was visiting his parents in Atlanta when he and Baldwin met.

The minister was in the middle of a hectic lecture tour, during which he had been organizing support for a national civil rights campaign. Yet he remained calm and cordial, deeply impressing Baldwin with his tremendous aura of inner peace and moral power. The author listened as King explained his political philosophy, which was based on the pacifist teachings of the Indian nationalist leader Mahatma Gandhi. The use of nonviolent protest activity to bring about social reform was an important part of King's civil rights campaign.

Baldwin decided to make a trip to Montgomery to hear King give a sermon at his church the following Sunday. Wanting to get a feel for the city, he flew to Montgomery a few days early. The first capital of the South during the Civil War, the city still had about it an air of the glory days of the Confederacy. Much about the town, including race relations, had remained virtually unchanged for nearly a century. But change had certainly come.

In 1956, this bastion of the Old South had been shaken by the black community's boycott of the city's segregated bus lines. Prior to the boycott, blacks had been confined by a city ordinance to the back section

The Reverend Martin Luther King, Jr., speaks to a crowd of supporters in Montgomery, Alabama, during his campaign to end segregation on city buses in 1956. "If you are cut down in a movement that is designed to save the soul of a nation, then no other death could be more redemptive," he said.

of buses. A federal court declared in 1957 that the segregation ordinance was unconstitutional and gave blacks the right to sit anywhere they pleased. When Baldwin arrived, he said he found the white population "baffled and demoralized" by the court's ruling.

Anxious to see whether the desegregation order was being obeyed, Baldwin decided to ride on a bus as soon as he got to Montgomery. He waited on line at a bus stop with other blacks and whites, boarding the first bus that came along. When he asked the white driver how much the fare was, the man merely gave him a hostile look and then turned away. Undaunted, Baldwin dropped 15 cents in the cash box and sat down a few seats forward of the center of the vehicle. He watched with satisfaction as other blacks boarded the bus and sat in the front seats.

On the following Sunday, Baldwin went to the worship services at the Dexter Avenue Baptist Church, where the pastor was the Reverend King. Immediately upon entering the red-brick building, the 33-year-old writer experienced a sensation that transcended anything he had ever felt in a church. The congregation at first looked like so many others that filled churches every Sunday: The children were scrubbed and immaculately dressed; the women displayed their Sunday finery; and the men appeared unusually reflective. But Baldwin also noticed distinct joy among those who packed King's church.

Baldwin was equally amazed by King's sermon. He had never heard a minister speak to his congregation the way King did. There were no Holy Roller verbal fireworks here. Instead, King directed his speech to the social problems faced by blacks and called on them to pursue a higher moral standard in order to overcome the crime, poverty, and other ills that devastated so many of their communities. King offered both praise and criticism to his parishioners, but his message was clear: We have got to do better, and we have got to take responsibility for our communities.

Civil rights activists in Birmingham, Alabama, sit at the front of a bus, officially reserved for whites only, to protest the city's discriminatory public transportation laws. One of the most startling changes Baldwin witnessed in his odyssey through the South in 1957 was the end of segregation on buses.

Baldwin had the chance to talk to King again at a church dinner after the service. He was impressed that the minister never once mentioned the recent bombings of his home and his church. Instead, King talked about the many courageous freedom fighters who were making enormous sacrifices to bring about equal opportunity for all Americans. The discussions with King convinced Baldwin that he should become personally involved in the civil rights movement.

Baldwin returned to New York shortly thereafter. He mused while walking around his predominantly white neighborhood in lower Manhattan that the whites around him were less familiar with blacks than were their white counterparts in the South. He realized that the battle against segregation would have to be waged in New York City almost as strongly as it was being fought in Montgomery.

During the late 1950s, Baldwin published many articles that contained his impressions of the South and its inhabitants. "I met the most beautiful people I ever met in my life down there," he wrote. "I mean Negro grocery men, for example, whose stores had been bombed. Who nevertheless went *on*. It was just incredible." He decided to pay tribute to these people in the best way he knew how—by writing about them. His essays on the South proved to be immensely popular, and they helped provide the American public with a clearer understanding of the terrors and triumphs that southern blacks had to face daily.

An essay on matters closer to home did not meet with the same kind of reception. Early in 1960, *Esquire* magazine commissioned Baldwin to write a lengthy article on Harlem. He took on the assignment with some trepidation, knowing that he would probably have to face some disturbing truths, just as he had when he wrote "The Harlem Ghetto" more than 20 years before.

When Baldwin entered his old neighborhood and revisited the street on which he had grown up, he was shocked to see how much it had changed. The area was now dubbed "Junkies' Hollow" because of the high volume of drug dealing that took place there. Everywhere, he saw destitute young people slumped over on the dirty sidewalks and sitting on stoops, staring vacantly into space. Harlem had degenerated beyond belief.

Approaching the site where his old tenement building once stood, Baldwin discovered that it had been replaced by a housing project. Made up of low-rent, high-rise apartment buildings for the poor, housing projects were usually subsidized by the city or federal government. Although they became a popular vehicle for social reform in the 1950s and 1960s, Baldwin believed that such projects were drab and characterless, thereby isolating residents from the surrounding community.

When Baldwin returned to his downtown apartment, he wrote a scathing article about what he had witnessed. He said that housing projects were "colorless, bleak, high, and revolting . . . a monument to the folly, and the cowardice, of good intentions." He even went so far as to call Riverton, a middle-class housing project in Harlem, a "slum." He ended his angry litany with the words: "Walk through the streets of Harlem and see what we, this nation, have become."

When the *Esquire* issue containing Baldwin's essay, entitled "Fifth Avenue, Uptown," hit the newsstands in July 1960, it was greeted with indignation by many Harlemites. Riverton's residents were especially angry, and they demanded that Baldwin retract his statements. Although he refused to do so, the backlash still upset him.

Baldwin's next writing venture, *Nobody Knows My Name: More Notes of a Native Son*, met with a far more popular response. The book was a collection of essays on Harlem and the South, and it did much to increase his stature as one of the most insightful

"This man," the writer Imamu Amiri Baraka said of Baldwin, "traveled the earth like its history and its biographer. He reported, criticized, made beautiful, analyzed, cajoled, lyricized, attacked, sang, made us think, made us better, made us consciously human."

Many black New Yorkers were outraged when Baldwin described Harlem's middle-class Riverton housing project (shown here) as a slum. He believed that massive urban housing complexes— whether for the poor or the rich— isolated their residents from the rest of the community.

spokesmen for the civil rights movement. The *Atlantic Monthly* said his words represented "the voice of a new generation."

Rarely content to remain in one place for very long, Baldwin gave up his apartment in New York and stayed for varying lengths of time at the homes of friends in America and abroad. He lived in such places as Connecticut, New Hampshire, France, and Turkey. His hosts marveled at his ability to stay up night after night, either working or carousing with the members of his entourage—a group of friends and acquaintances who seemed to appear like magic wherever he was staying. A tireless talker who thrived on the company of others, he almost never spent a quiet evening alone.

From 1960 to 1962, Baldwin maintained a heavy schedule of lecturing and writing. By this time, the royalties he was earning from his books had grown substantially, and he was able to treat the members of his family to the luxuries they could never afford when he was growing up. In 1961, he took his youngest sister, 18-year-old Paula Maria, on a tour of Paris. The next year, he and his sister Gloria traveled to

Africa to celebrate the fifth anniversary of Ghana's independence. Baldwin was fascinated to discover that many of the people he met there reminded him, at least vaguely, of friends in America. Women in Ghana, he said, "had a certain *style* which I recognized. From somewhere, from Harlem."

In June 1962, Baldwin published his third novel, *Another Country*. A biting, furious story of prejudice and betrayal, the book revolves around the last days of jazz drummer Rufus Scott. It is full of life, yet it failed to receive the enthusiastic reviews his two previous novels had elicited.

For a brief period, Baldwin was demoralized. But when an interviewer from the *New York Post* asked him about the book, he became defiantly philosophical. "No matter what critics say," he told the reporter, "a writer knows if he's done his best. . . . This may be a failure, but it's not a lie." As it turned out, the reading public disagreed with the critics, and *Another Country* became a national best-seller.

Baldwin's publisher promoted the book with an extravagant publication party at the author's favorite Harlem night spot, Small's Paradise. Sipping scotch and tapping his feet to the music, the 37-year-old author watched the place fill to capacity with celebrities and important writers. As the evening wore on, he talked to nearly everyone in the room and then joined the more active revelers on the dance floor, gyrating to a new dance called the Twist. It was his idea of a perfect evening. ☙

7

"THE FIRE
NEXT TIME!"

❧

IN THE EARLY 1960s, Baldwin became increasingly caught up in the civil rights movement. He frequently spent long periods outside of New York, making speeches and doing research for magazine articles about the struggle for racial justice. Everywhere he traveled, he saw blacks forging a new political identity. As a group, they were beginning to demand their rightful place in American society and taking steps to shape the future of race relations in the country.

Like the Reverend Martin Luther King, Jr., Baldwin believed that the best way to improve social conditions for blacks was to use nonviolent protest methods to gather popular support for racial integration and equal opportunity. During his travels, the author met with political activists and clergymen whose views differed sharply from those advocated by King and other mainstream civil rights leaders. Some of these black leaders believed that the struggle for racial freedom had to be pursued with more radical methods than protest marches and prayer meetings.

Two of the most outspoken of the militant black activists who emerged in the early 1960s were the

Baldwin at the Lincoln Memorial during the March on Washington for Jobs and Freedom, a civil rights demonstration held in August 1963. He is surrounded by (left to right) the actors Charlton Heston, Harry Belafonte, and Marlon Brando.

Elijah Muhammad, the spiritual leader of the Nation of Islam, called on blacks to reject their ties to white society and Christianity. Baldwin's meeting with the Black Muslim leader in 1962 served as the focal point of his book The Fire Next Time.

Black Muslim leaders Elijah Muhammad and Malcolm X. Preaching that blacks were morally and biologically superior to whites and that God—or Allah, as he is known to Muslims—was preparing to annihilate the "degenerate" white race, Muhammad and Malcolm X succeeded in drawing thousands of members to their religious sect, the Nation of Islam. A fiery and inspirational speaker, Malcolm X called for blacks to reject racial integration and to use any means—whether violent or nonviolent—to found a separate black nation. The Muslim preacher was distrustful of any black leader who worked with whites to bring about social change, and he accused King and his fellow integrationists of being white men's slaves.

Although Baldwin rejected the Black Muslims' extremist views, he supported their attempts to foster black pride and independence. Like Malcolm X, his roots were in America's black ghettos, and he was familiar with the various factors that led to the Muslim leader's anger and bitterness. Baldwin had another thing in common with Malcolm X: He believed that the Nation of Islam was a force with which to be reckoned.

In 1962, Baldwin received an invitation from Elijah Muhammad to visit the Black Muslims' national headquarters in Chicago. He was surprised at the offer because the Muslims knew he was committed to uniting blacks and whites in an effort to gain racial understanding. Nevertheless, he quickly accepted Muhammad's invitation. The writer in Baldwin was too curious to turn down such an extraordinary offer. He was especially interested in seeing how the Muslims, whose religious beliefs did not permit them to use alcohol or tobacco and who believed that homosexuality was evil, would deal with his habits and views.

Immediately upon presenting himself at the entrance of the Nation of Islam's headquarters, Baldwin felt as if he had been summoned to appear before royalty: Everyone's bearing seemed so dignified. He was led into a room occupied by several women in white gowns and a few men wearing dark suits. When Elijah Muhammad finally appeared, Baldwin was stunned. He had expected the Muslim leader to be fierce and imposing. Instead, he was small and slender, with a delicate face and a kindly manner.

The interview between Baldwin and Muhammad took place at dinner, during which the author sat next to the Muslim leader, in the place of honor. It began with Baldwin nervously gulping down two glasses of milk set before him while he waited for Muhammad to speak. After several minutes, Muhammad mentioned he had recently seen Baldwin on television, being interviewed by what the Black Muslim called "white devils." In fact, most of his caustic comments were directed at whites. These attacks made Baldwin increasingly uncomfortable. Finally, he said he had many white friends whom he loved and respected. Upon hearing this, Muhammad gave him a look of great pity.

When the meeting was over, Muhammad walked his guest to the front door. Together, they looked out at the city streets. It was an unsettling moment, Baldwin later said, for it made him think: "Because of the reality of and the nature of those streets—because of what [Muhammad] conceived as his responsibility and what I took to be mine—we would always be strangers, and possibly, one day, enemies."

Baldwin collected this and other thoughts about the Black Muslims and the future of race relations in America into what was to become perhaps his most famous essay, "Letter from a Region in My Mind." It was originally published in the *New Yorker* magazine in November 1962 and was reprinted in book form two months later under the book title *The Fire Next Time*. Apparently, the public agreed with Lang-

The radical Black Muslim minister Malcolm X waged a relentless battle to ignite a political revolution in the streets of America's black ghettos. "The masses of black people," he proclaimed, "want a society of their own in a land of their own."

ston Hughes's appraisal that "few American writers handle words more effectively in the essay form than James Baldwin." The book quickly became a national best-seller.

A characteristically hard-hitting personal testament to the author's lifelong battle against racial oppression, *The Fire Next Time* shocked many Americans. Baldwin's grim assessment of the state of the country's racial situation left him without any doubts that a major cataclysm loomed ahead unless blacks and whites learned to live together. In the prophetically titled book, he warned, "If we do not now dare everything, the fulfillment of that prophecy, recreated from the Bible in song by a slave, is upon us: *God gave Noah the rainbow sign, No more water, the fire next time!*"

Baldwin argued that although a rising tide of black militancy was already beginning to transform America, the answer to the country's problems did not lie in black separatism. The black man, he said, "had been formed by the nation, for better or for worse, and does not belong to any other—not to Africa, and certainly not to Islam." For those who looked to either the Nation of Islam or the Ku Klux Klan for solutions, he gave this warning: "The glorification of one race and the consequent debasement of another—or others—always has been and always will be a recipe for murder."

The publication of *The Fire Next Time* helped Baldwin's fame reach its zenith, and he was immediately booked for lecture appearances across the country. Before embarking on the tour, he decided to make a trip to Jackson, Mississippi, to meet two special people. His first appointment was with James Meredith, a black air force veteran who had won a court battle in 1962 that allowed him to become the first black student ever to attend the University of Mississippi. Baldwin listened in awe as Meredith de-

James Meredith (center) is escorted to class by federal marshals during his successful effort to desegregate the University of Mississippi. Baldwin met with Meredith and civil rights activist Medgar Evers in the fall of 1962.

scribed what it was like to enter an all-white university while a mob of segregationists attacked the troops who were escorting him to class.

After spending three days with Meredith, Baldwin visited Medgar Evers, the leader of the NAACP's civil rights forces in Jackson. At the time, Evers was investigating the murder of a black man by a white storekeeper in a nearby town. Baldwin accompanied Evers on his dangerous treks into the Mississippi backwoods and took notes about the case, which he later used as the inspiration for a play, *Blues for Mister Charlie*. Deeply impressed by the courageous Evers, Baldwin said, "He had the calm of somebody who knows he's going to die." Tragically, Evers was murdered by white racists three months after his meeting with Baldwin.

Baldwin began a speaking tour of the South and the West after his visits with Meredith and Evers. While in California, he learned that Martin Luther King was planning to lead a massive civil rights campaign in Birmingham, Alabama, beginning in April. Birmingham was known as one of the most racially oppressive cities in the nation, situated in a state whose governor, George Wallace, had been sworn into office pledging, "Segregation now! Segregation tomorrow! Segregation forever!" In fact, King called

Birmingham "the most segregated city in the United States."

On April 3, King issued the "Birmingham Manifesto," a document that listed the demands of his civil rights campaign. The manifesto called for the desegregation of lunch counters and rest rooms and for the hiring of more blacks in local industry. During the next month, King and his chief associates, Ralph Abernathy and Fred Shuttlesworth, organized sit-ins and protest marches throughout the city. The police force, directed by Sheriff Bull Connor, made savage attacks on the demonstrators, beating and arresting hundreds of them. King himself was arrested during a prayer demonstration and jailed for more than a week.

By the time King posted bond and was released from jail, the Birmingham protest campaign had begun to falter. But then, in a surprising develop-

A policeman uses an attack dog to break up a civil rights demonstration in Birmingham, Alabama. "Here in Birmingham we have reached the point of no return," announced the Reverend Martin Luther King, Jr., in April 1963, as he launched a massive campaign against racial discrimination.

ment, hundreds of black students appeared before King and asked his permission to hold a "Children's Crusade" through the streets of Birmingham. Though reluctant to risk the lives of the students, King finally decided that the sight of the marching children might capture America's sympathy for the civil rights movement. He prayed that the police would leave the children alone.

King's prayers were not answered. On May 2, as 1,000 young demonstrators clapped their hands and sang while marching through the streets, they were surrounded by police and arrested. Undaunted by the arrests, more than 2,500 students turned out to march the next day. Infuriated, Sheriff Connor ordered his men to unleash their attack dogs and to fire jets of water on the demonstrators. Scores of children were knocked unconscious by the blasts from the hoses. Others were mauled by the dogs.

A wave of revulsion swept across America on the evening of May 3, when television broadcasts showed the fate of the Children's Crusade. President John F. Kennedy was also angered by the actions of the Birmingham police, and he sent U.S. assistant attorney general Burke Marshall to Birmingham to arrange a truce in the city. The calm was broken when the bombing of King's headquarters on May 11 sparked a night of rioting in the city.

Baldwin, who had followed these events closely, cabled U.S. attorney general Robert Kennedy on May 12 to complain that the president was not doing enough to stop the violence. On the same day, President Kennedy ordered 3,000 troops into the city and made plans to mobilize the National Guard. As a result, a very fragile truce held the city together for the next several days while the Kennedys searched frantically for a way to end the troubles in Birmingham and to keep them from sparking racial violence in other cities.

At a 1963 press conference in New York City, Baldwin and civil rights activist Bayard Rustin express their outrage about the murder of four black children in Birmingham.

On the following Sunday, May 17, Baldwin was featured on the cover of *Time* magazine. His photograph appeared in conjunction with an article on his role in the civil rights movement. The *Time* article heaped praise on the best-selling author, stating, "There is not another writer, white or black, who expresses with such poignancy and abrasiveness the dark realities of the racial ferment in North and South."

Five days later, Baldwin was on his way to a lecture engagement at Wesleyan University in Middletown, Connecticut, when he received a message that Robert Kennedy had been trying to reach him on the telephone. He was instantly wary. Perhaps, he figured, the attorney general wanted to enlist his help in an effort to calm the racial tensions in the country.

At that very moment, King was threatening to unleash massive, nationwide protests if a proposed civil rights bill was not passed by Congress. Baldwin was not sure whether the Kennedy administration was committed to supporting the bill and aiding the civil rights movement, and he wondered whether he would wind up hurting the cause by assisting the attorney general. After mulling over the question, he returned Robert Kennedy's call and accepted an invitation to meet with the attorney general the next morning at his private estate in McLean, Virginia.

On May 23, the proud, streetwise author from the Harlem ghetto sat down to breakfast with the wealthy, Harvard-educated attorney general. Over poached eggs and coffee, Kennedy quizzed Baldwin about the political goals of various black rights organizations. He fired off question after question: "How important do you think the Black Muslims are?" "Who are the Negroes other Negroes listen to?" He wanted to know who Baldwin thought had the best solutions for addressing the chronic problems that plagued minority groups. Baldwin answered the questions as best he could.

U.S. attorney general Robert Kennedy addresses a crowd at a civil rights demonstration in Washington, D.C., in 1963. Baldwin's angry telegram to Kennedy on the day after the Birmingham riot initiated a political summit between the two men.

Next, Kennedy asked if Baldwin could bring together a group of prominent blacks who would be willing to discuss these matters further. Baldwin agreed, and the two set a date for their black-white "summit meeting." It was scheduled to be held at the attorney general's apartment in New York.

Back in Manhattan, Baldwin set to work inviting a dozen associates to the upcoming meeting with Kennedy. A few of them were skeptical about the conference and wanted to know whether Kennedy would really listen to their views. Despite their questions, Baldwin managed to recruit a diverse and illustrious group of activists, politicians, educators, and entertainers. Among them were singers Lena Horne and Harry Belafonte, playwright Lorraine Hansberry, and psychologist Kenneth Clark.

The meeting did not go well, however. The highly charged group of civil rights supporters criticized the Kennedy administration for not doing more to improve conditions for blacks. Robert Kennedy, on the other hand, was surprised that his guests did believe the government was making a major effort to support the civil rights movement. Somewhat offended by their attitude, Kennedy ended the meeting as quickly as possible.

Baldwin's worries that the meeting might have dampened Robert Kennedy's enthusiasm for the civil rights movement proved groundless. He remained sympathetic to King and other blacks clamoring for change and urged his brother to support attempts to desegregate the South. The demonstrations in Birmingham had already resulted in one major victory: It was agreed that For Whites Only signs would be taken down from rest rooms, drinking fountains, restaurants, and swimming pools in the city.

In an effort to see the tokens of Jim Crow removed in other cities as well, President Kennedy went on national television on the night of June 11, 1963, and called for an end to segregation. "We are confronted primarily with a moral issue," he told the nation. "Those who do nothing are inviting shame as well as violence. Those who act boldly are recognizing right as well as reality." The following week, he submitted a sweeping civil rights bill to Congress, touching off a fierce and acrimonious debate on Capitol Hill as southern congressmen battled to keep the bill from passing.

That same month, Baldwin took a break from his political activities for a reunion with Richard Avedon, one of his friends from high school. Avedon had received an assignment from *Harper's Bazaar* magazine to photograph his former classmate, and during the course of the shooting, the two decided to collaborate on a book of photo essays. They flew to Puerto Rico to work on the project.

Ensconced in a small fishing village, the writer and the photographer prepared the text and illustrations for their book, which was published the following year as *Nothing Personal*. "It was exactly the way we used to work at school," Avedon recalled. "I kept thinking, 'Here we are back in the tower.' "

After Baldwin finished his work with Avedon, he decided to remain in Puerto Rico and invite his entire family to join him for a week's vacation. For Baldwin, the family gathering was like the fulfillment of a dream. During his childhood, he used to fantasize about taking his family in "a big Buick car" to his own house in the country.

One night, everyone in the family stayed up late, acting out the parts in Baldwin's nearly completed new play, *Blues for Mister Charlie*. The playwright's mother proved to be the hit of the evening. Her gift for dramatic reading astonished all of her children.

The public treated the play less kindly. *Blues for Mister Charlie*, a bitter story about a down-and-out jazz musician who returns to his birthplace in the South and is murdered, received mixed reviews when it opened on Broadway the following year. Baldwin's lone compensation was the fact that his brother David was cast in one of the lead roles.

After his Caribbean vacation, Baldwin returned to Paris, all the while continuing to follow the American political scene as closely as possible. Late in the summer, he heard about a new civil rights offensive. A giant demonstration, called the March on Washington for Jobs and Freedom, was scheduled to take place in the nation's capital on August 28.

Baldwin decided that Americans in Paris should take part in the civil rights campaign. He organized a contingent of his friends to march in support of the upcoming demonstration. On August 21, more than 500 black and white Americans filed along Parisian boulevards to the U.S. embassy. There the group handed an embassy official a petition that expressed their desire to "eradicate all racial barriers in American life [and] to liberate all Americans from the prison of their biases and fears."

Even though his rally in Paris had been a success, Baldwin could not stay away from the march in Washington. On August 27, he flew back to the United States. The next day, he joined 250,000 other march-

Baldwin speaks to a group of American musicians who held a rally in Paris in support of the March on Washington for Jobs and Freedom. The group signed a petition that praised the efforts of the civil rights movement "to liberate all Americans from the prison of their biases and fears."

On August 28, 1963, Baldwin joined more than 250,000 supporters of the civil rights movement for a demonstration of unity in Washington, D.C. After the rally, the crowd listened to the Reverend Martin Luther King, Jr., issue a stirring cry, "From every mountainside, let freedom ring."

ers in a long procession that filed past the White House. Then he sat with a group of prominent figures on the speakers' platform in front of the Lincoln Memorial. One by one, the people on the platform paraded to the microphone and addressed the crowd.

Baldwin listened to labor leader A. Philip Randolph start off the day's orations by telling the assembly, "Let the nation and the world know the meaning of our numbers." Like most of the demonstrators, Baldwin could only marvel at the size of the crowd gathered before him. Later on, he had the opportunity to offer them a short, congratulatory speech and to hear King reach out to the audience with the ringing words, "I have a dream."

The hopes that were raised on August 28 were soon tempered by a series of violent acts. In September, four black children were killed by a bomb planted in a church in Birmingham. Two months later, on November 22, President Kennedy was assassinated in Dallas, Texas. Coupled with the murder of Medgar Evers the previous June, these tragedies cast a pall over the civil rights movement.

The loss of Kennedy, whom many blacks viewed as a champion of racial progress, was considered an especially grievous blow. Baldwin had been critical of Kennedy on numerous occasions. Yet he praised the late president as someone who was willing to listen to the voices of people in the black ghettos.

As the reins of power passed from Kennedy to his successor, Lyndon Johnson, the political climate of the country began to change. Racial tensions increased, leading to a series of riots in 1964 that devastated several American cities. It was the violent storm that Baldwin had predicted was going to whip through America.

Nevertheless, Baldwin held out hope for the future. He had written in the introduction to *The Fire Next Time*, "This is your home, my friend, do not be driven from it; great men have done great things here, and will again, and we can make America what America must become." Only now it was time for such promises to be delivered. ✤

8

A TIME FOR DREAMS

ONE MORNING IN January 1965, Baldwin was sitting at his typewriter when he was interrupted by the ring of his telephone. It was a friend on the line, calling to let him know that the Reverend Martin Luther King, Jr., was getting ready to tackle the issue of racial discrimination in Selma, Alabama. Would Baldwin, his friend wanted to know, be willing to appear at a massive protest demonstration that was planned for March? The writer agreed to cut short a scheduled trip to England and attend the rally.

King's campaign in Selma was part of a nationwide effort by black groups to pressure President Johnson into supporting stronger voting-rights legislation for minority groups. In the Deep South, an estimated 72 percent of voting-age blacks were unable to cast a ballot because of discriminatory state laws that required them to pass a literacy test. Many eligible voters were disqualified from voting thanks to such minor technicalities as failing to cross the letter *t* on a registration form. King knew that if a voting-rights bill were passed in Congress, 2 million blacks might get the chance to vote for the first time in their life.

Baldwin speaks to a crowd gathered on the steps of the Alabama state capitol building following the civil rights march from Selma to Montgomery in March 1965. To the right of him are civil rights leaders Bayard Rustin and A. Philip Randolph.

*Black residents of a rural Ala-
bama town line up to register to
vote. In the mid-1960s, blacks in
the South gained a greater say in
their future as President Lyndon
Johnson and Congress stepped up
efforts to ban discriminatory laws
that had been used to keep blacks
from voting.*

King touched off the campaign in Selma with a series of marches that began in January 1965. His goal was not only to publicize abuses in the voting registration requirements but also to inform blacks about the importance of registering to vote. The Selma campaign became a symbol of the black struggle for political power in the South.

During a march early in the campaign, King was arrested and thrown in jail. When his wife, Coretta, visited him two days later, she brought some astonishing news: Malcolm X had come to Selma to support the campaign. The Muslim activist had recently separated from the Nation of Islam and had founded his own radical organization called Muslim Mosque, Incorporated. He was no longer opposed to King's nonviolent protest methods. He was willing to accept any means that would help bring about revolutionary changes in conditions for blacks. "It's a time for martyrs now," he said. "And if I'm to be one, it will be in the cause of brotherhood. That's the only thing that can save this country. I've learned it the hard way—but I've learned it."

Baldwin was in Cambridge, England, when he heard about Malcolm X's conciliatory gesture toward the leaders of the civil rights movement, and the news greatly pleased him. He believed that the radical Muslim preacher was one of most farsighted of black leaders. He hoped that King and Malcolm X could unite forces behind a campaign for black rights.

The next news that Baldwin heard from Selma was not so pleasing. During a demonstration in early February, a column of students was set upon by the police force of Sheriff Jim Clark, who used electric cattle prods to break up the march. It sickened Baldwin to hear about the incident, and he told a group of Cambridge University students, "I suggest that what has happened to the white Southerner is in some ways much worse than what has happened to the Negroes there. . . . One has to assume he is a man like me, but he does not know what drives him to use the club, to menace with the gun and to use a cattle prod against a woman's breasts. . . . Their moral lives have been destroyed by a plague called color."

Baldwin continued to air his views during a formal debate. This highly publicized event took place at Cambridge University before a packed house. The crowd was anxious to hear the 41-year-old writer go head to head with the noted American journalist William F. Buckley on the topic of "The American Dream and the American Negro." Baldwin's opponent, the editor of the *National Review*, a conservative political journal, was white, and he was renowned for his eloquence and formidable intellect. It was said that he rarely lost an argument.

Baldwin was known to be just as eloquent, however, and he did not disappoint the audience. He opened the debate with a resounding salvo. "I am not a ward of America, I am not an object of missionary charity," he said. "I am one of the people who built the country. . . . I picked cotton, I carried it to the market, I built the railroads under someone else's whip for nothing. For nothing!"

At once magisterial and pugnacious, Baldwin quickly moved on to other topics. He said about the atrocities that were occurring in the South, "This is not being done 100 years ago, but in 1965 and in a country . . . that calls itself a civilized nation and which espouses the notion of freedom in the world!" By this time, he was riding high on a wave of indignant oratory, much to the delight of his audience. "Until the moment comes," he continued, "when we, the Americans, are able to accept the fact that my ancestors are both black and white, that on the continent we are trying to forge a new identity, that we need each other, that I am *not* a ward of America . . . until this moment comes there is scarcely any hope for the American dream."

When Baldwin was through with his opening attack, Buckley attempted to respond with a vigorous defense of America's political order. He attacked Baldwin as a "posturing hero" who should be ashamed of his "flagellations of our civilization." The students, however, sided with Baldwin, voting him the winner of the debate by an overwhelming majority.

Baldwin's pleasure over his triumph in the Cambridge debate was short lived. A week later, while still in England, he learned that Malcolm X had been shot while giving a political address in Harlem. Less than two and a half weeks after he uttered his prophetic statement about martyrdom, Malcolm X was dead. Three men with connections to the Nation of Islam were later convicted of the murder, but many people who studied the case doubted that the real assassins had been caught.

Within hours of Malcolm X's assassination on February 21, reporters flocked to Baldwin to get his response to the killing. As they shoved microphones near him, the distraught Baldwin nearly lost control of himself. He screamed at the group, "You did it! It is because of you—the men who created this white

supremacy—that this man is dead. You are not guilty—but you did it!"

Two weeks later, as Baldwin prepared to return to the States, he learned that more acts of racial violence had shaken the nation. On March 7, 1965, the Selma police went on a rampage that resulted in the hospitalization of 80 marchers. This time, the brutality of Sheriff Clark's men was presented on all the major television news broadcasts. One of the networks, ABC, even interrupted its Sunday night movie to show film footage of what was being called "Bloody Sunday." The sheriff's reign of terror sparked

"He is thought-provoking, tantalizing, irritating, abusing and amusing," the poet Langston Hughes said of Baldwin. *"And he uses words as the sea uses waves, to flow and beat, advance and retreat, rise and take a bow in disappearing."*

As part of the Reverend Martin Luther King, Jr.'s efforts to win voting-rights legislation, civil rights demonstrators in Selma, Alabama, confront a row of state troopers in March 1965. Later in the month, Baldwin joined King in Montgomery, Alabama, at the tail end of a five-day protest march that began in Selma.

waves of protest across the country, and race riots erupted in a number of cities.

These events tipped the scales for the Johnson administration, which was working on a new piece of legislation to guarantee blacks the right to vote. On March 15, the president appeared before Congress to announce his full support for a proposed voting-rights bill. "This time, on this issue, there must be no delay," Johnson said in his address, which was carried on national television. "Their cause must be our cause, too."

Johnson's announcement did not stop King's plans to hold a five-day-long protest march from Selma to Montgomery. On Sunday, March 21, thousands of King's supporters gathered for the beginning of the march. Walking by day and camping at night, the throng advanced toward the Alabama state capital. Four days later, Baldwin and more than 40,000 other civil rights sympathizers met the marchers just before their triumphant entry into Montgomery.

After paying his respects to King, Baldwin joined the procession, taking the hand of folksinger Joan Baez. Led by two flag bearers—one black and one white—and a man playing "Yankee Doodle" on a fife, the marchers pushed on through torrents of rain. By the time they reached Montgomery, the rain had ended, and the column of thousands—clapping hands, singing songs, and waving flags—entered the capital in a flood of sunlight.

On the night of March 25, a crowd of 10,000 people gathered in a rain-soaked ball park to celebrate the completion of the march. On the speakers' podium, Baldwin sat next to Harry Belafonte, composer Leonard Bernstein, and numerous other celebrities. When it was his turn to speak, Baldwin congratulated the marchers on their spirited show of unity. After the speeches, the folksinging trio of Peter, Paul, and Mary led the crowd in a moving rendition of Bob Dylan's "Blowin' in the Wind," which had become one of the anthems of the 1960s.

The highlight of the evening in Montgomery occurred when King appeared on the podium, his pants legs rolled up above his hiking boots. "What do you want?" he yelled at the crowd. "Freedom!" they shouted back. "When do you want it?" King asked. The marchers responded, "Now!"

The Selma-to-Montgomery march was a success. In August, Congress passed the Voting Rights Act, a piece of iron-toothed legislation that outlawed the use of literacy tests in determining voter eligibility and set up federal supervision of registration and polling offices in the South. President Johnson called the law a "triumph for freedom as huge as any victory that's ever been won on a battlefield."

But while the Johnson administration was signing civil rights bills, it was also embroiling the nation ever more deeply in a bloody conflict in Southeast Asia. As marchers were making their way to Alabama's capital in March 1965, the first U.S. combat troops were landing on the shores of Vietnam. By August, troop strength totaled in the hundreds of thousands.

Baldwin was among those who severely criticized U.S. participation in the Vietnam War, which he believed was an immoral waste of lives and national resources. The war aroused waves of protest that swelled dramatically during the next nine years of American participation. During that time, war protestors joined ranks with civil rights activists and other social reformers. Spearheaded by the burgeoning antiwar movement, a loose coalition of activist groups worked to bring about sweeping changes in American society. "Make love, not war!"; "Burn your draft card!"; "Give students a voice, not a gun!"; and "Black Power now!" were just a few of the slogans that helped set the political climate.

Changes occurred in the civil rights movement as well. Voices of moderation gradually gave way to increasingly radical calls for change. Even the vocabulary was different. The terms "Afro-American" and "black" were considered preferable to two previously widely used terms: "Negro" and "colored."

Among the heralds of the new political activism was a group of young firebrands with their own visions of justice. Militants such as Stokely Carmichael, the leader of the Student Nonviolent Coordinating Committee (SNCC), and Eldridge Cleaver, cofounder of the radical Black Panther party, called for the violent overthrow of the old political order and the establishment of separate white and black societies. In doing so, they sparred verbally with Baldwin, King, and others they viewed as moderates.

Baldwin was shocked when Cleaver, the author of a best-selling political treatise, *Soul on Ice*, attacked his writing. The Black Panther leader labeled Baldwin's work "the most shameful, sycophantic love of whites that one can find in the writings of any black American writer of note in our time." More saddened than angered by Cleaver's attack, Baldwin responded that he sympathized with the Panthers' goals of raising black consciousness but objected to the violent methods they proposed to gain political power.

"Power without morality," Baldwin said, "is no longer power." He went on to prophesy, rather astutely, "A great deal of what passes for black militancy right now is nothing but a fashion. . . . What is important is the impulse out of which it has come and which it reveals. And what's valuable in it will remain, and the rest will go."

Baldwin was given an equally hard time by the black activist and writer LeRoi Jones (who later changed his name to Imamu Amiri Baraka). An outspoken leader of the new Black Arts movement,

Stokely Carmichael, head of the Student Nonviolent Coordinating Committee, was one of several radical black leaders who disagreed with Baldwin's political views. Despite his organization's passive-sounding name, Carmichael called for a violent revolution to overthrow America's existing political order.

Baldwin and 300,000 other mourners, including the Reverend Jesse Jackson (top row, second from left), attended the Reverend Martin Luther King, Jr.'s funeral in Atlanta on April 9, 1968. King's assassination proved to be a decisive blow to the civil rights movement.

which championed art in the service of a political cause, Jones severely criticized Baldwin, finding his writings to be "white-tainted." Baldwin responded to this charge by stating that his frequent use of white protagonists in his novels was part of an attempt to explore all sides of the issue in determining who is responsible for racial oppression.

Baldwin's tussles with his critics within the Black Power movement were part of a general trend toward disunity within the civil rights movement in the late 1960s. In the midst of this infighting, another tragedy occurred. On the evening of April 4, 1968, King was assassinated. He was gunned down by a white man named James Earl Ray while standing on the balcony of his hotel room in Memphis, Tennessee, where he had gone to support a march of striking sanitation workers seeking higher wages.

On April 9, a grief-stricken Baldwin attended the funeral service for King in Atlanta, Georgia. More than 300,000 mourners followed the mule-drawn cart that carried King's body to the cemetery; around the nation, 120 million Americans watched the service on television. Speaking before the assembled crowd, King's chief assistant, Ralph Abernathy, described the time as "one of the darkest in the history of the black people of this nation . . . one of the darkest hours in the history of all mankind."

A short time after the funeral, Coretta Scott King gave Baldwin a wristwatch on whose face was a portrait of her husband along with the stirring words that King had spoken at the March on Washington in 1963: "I have a dream." Like the revered leader of the civil rights struggle, Baldwin refused to accept a world filled with angry passion. "To hate, to be violent, is demeaning," he said. The only lasting way to foster racial understanding, according to Baldwin, was through the all-healing power of fellowship and love.

9
AND
A TIME
OF PEACE

I N THE GENTLE breeze of an early August afternoon in 1979, bird songs carried tranquil notes across a nearby meadow. An abundance of yellow wildflowers signaled summer's end. In an old stone farmhouse, Baldwin was sleeping off the effects of an all-night revel.

With a start, the reclining writer awoke and reached for his alarm clock. Seeing the hands pointing to 1:30 P.M., he wondered how he could have slept away the morning.

After dressing quickly, Baldwin descended a flight of stairs and headed for the kitchen. He revived himself with a generous cup of *café au lait*, a concoction of strong coffee and warmed milk. He took the coffee with him as he walked outside, into the sunshine, and seated himself in one of several dilapidated chairs arranged in a semicircle. The tightly cemented walls of his farmhouse let through none of the damp country air that chilled him to the core every winter and early spring but would be welcome on this sunbaked afternoon, and he thought back a bit wistfully to those

Baldwin spent many of his later years at his home in St. Paul de Vence in southern France. He said, "It was ironical to reflect that if I had not lived in France for so long I would never have found it necessary—or possible—to visit the American South."

cooler seasons. At this time of year, every part of nature seemed to him to be linked in a conspiracy to make him feel as hot as possible. At least, he reasoned, here in St. Paul de Vence, a village in southern France, he had escaped the oppressive heat of the New York City summer.

As Baldwin sipped his coffee, he reflected on the events of the night before. It had been a typical evening for him. Several of his friends had stopped by the farmhouse: the usual mix of artists and writers, vacationing Parisians, and acquaintances from America. He had coaxed some of them to join him for dinner at his favorite restaurant in the village, the Colombe d'Or. He liked the chef there, who always joked with him and pampered him with French delicacies and impeccable service. After dining on oysters, roast quail, chocolate mousse, and generous quantities of champagne and wine, the group had returned to Baldwin's house for nightcaps.

The evening and early morning had disappeared in the company of his friends. It was no wonder he was tired, he thought. But now he had to heave himself out of his chair and get to work, because tonight he was throwing a big party for himself: a birthday dinner of real American soul food. In the company of his friends, he would celebrate having just turned 55 years old.

During the past 11 years, Baldwin had learned how to balance his love of socializing with his passion for writing. He lived in a comfortable, even somewhat grand, style. A constant traveler, he maintained residences in various places around the world, including the south of France (which served as his main home), Paris, Istanbul, and New York City. His apartment in New York, which was located on the Upper West Side of Manhattan, was so large that he dubbed it "the barn." He often shared the huge space with family members.

Baldwin also dressed and ate in style. Most of his suits were hand tailored, he entertained lavishly, and he ate in the finest restaurants when he was not at more modest dining places feasting on his favorite soul food. When living in France, he sometimes traveled as far as 90 miles to savor the taste of venison prepared by a master chef. His frugal mother scolded him for his flamboyance, even chiding him for hailing a taxi instead of using the New York subways.

Although Baldwin indulged his own extravagances, he was also generous to his friends and to strangers who appealed to him for help. Whenever he returned to New York after a trip overseas, he immediately invited friends to one of the small restaurants in Harlem that served such southern delicacies as fried chicken, pigs' feet, chitterlings, and hominy grits. He almost always footed the bill in these and fancier places. On many occasions, he gave money to ballerinas, poets, and artists who were struggling to get through school and pay their rent. He often let aspiring artists stay in his apartment, even though the lodgers sometimes stole from him. He shrugged off such transgressions with good-natured understanding.

Baldwin's socializing and political activity did not always leave him as much time for writing as he wished. Sometimes, he stayed away from his typewriter for weeks and months. But when he returned to it, he was like a prodigal son, looking for forgiveness and renewal. "When the storm has settled," he said, "I do have a typewriter, which is my torment, but is also my work." Like many writers, he dealt with the anxiety of returning to work by sharpening pencils or by cleaning his apartment before committing the first word to paper. Once he settled down, however, he worked intensely for hours, usually until a phone call pulled him away to a press conference or a political gathering.

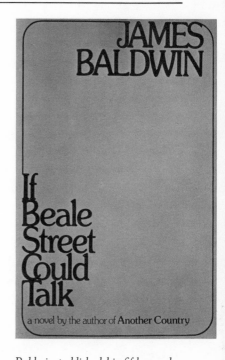

Baldwin published his fifth novel, If Beale Street Could Talk, *in 1974. Although his later novels generally lacked the power of his first works of fiction, his essays on the South in the 1980s continued to win critical acclaim.*

As the United States passed from the violent social upheavals of the Vietnam War era to the more
staid years of the late 1970s, Baldwin began to write
at a feverish pace. A short story collection, *Going to
Meet the Man*, was published in 1965 and was followed
by the novel *Tell Me How Long the Train's Been Gone*
in 1968; a dialogue with the anthropologist Margaret
Mead entitled *A Rap on Race* in 1971; two books of
essays, *No Name in the Street* and *One Day When I
Was Lost*, in 1972; *A Dialogue* (with the black poet
Nikki Giovanni) in 1973; the novel *If Beale Street
Could Talk* in 1974; and a book of essays, *The Devil
Finds Work*, in 1976.

In his later works, Baldwin continued to explore
the questions and issues that had interested him since
he was a struggling young writer in Greenwich Village. He took incisive looks at the role of prejudice
and self-deception in shaping an individual's identity.
In *A Rap on Race*, he once again talked about the
destruction caused by society's prejudice against minority groups. "It's difficult to be born, difficult to
learn to walk, difficult to grow old, difficult to die
and difficult to live for everybody, everywhere, forever," he wrote. "But no one has the right to put on
top of that another burden, another price which nobody can pay, and a burden which really nobody can
bear."

It was an issue that Baldwin tackled again and
again in his books. In *A Dialogue*, he said, "Let us
say . . . I can't get a job. . . . I mean, how in the
world, if I can't get a job, if I can't even get my sax
out of the pawnshop, if I can't even get the money
to get on the subway, how am I going to love anybody,
except in such an awful pain and rage that nobody
could bear it?"

At the age of 55, Baldwin still retained the ability
to entrance the public with his power and vision. In
the fall of 1979, he received word of the critical
acclaim his latest novel, *Just Above My Head*, was

receiving in New York. This sprawling work, which he dedicated to his brothers and sisters, embraces many of the topics that had become characteristic of his work: preachers, jazz, homosexual love, black pride, and the redeeming nature of love that is given unselfishly. One critic described the novel as "the work of a born storyteller at the height of his powers."

Later in 1979, Baldwin received a commission from *Esquire* magazine to write a story about the current state of race relations in the South. For the first time since his initial visit in 1957, he made an extended trip there. In planning his itinerary, he decided to spend most of his time in Birmingham, Alabama, the city where the members of the Children's Crusade had encountered Sheriff Connor's officers and dogs 16 years earlier.

While in Birmingham, Baldwin visited a courtroom in which a white man was being tried for the bombing of a black church in 1957. Looking around the room, Baldwin noticed a significant change from the recent past: The hall of justice was desegregated. Blacks and whites worked together with little sign of tension. But the change ended there. "We were surrounded," he wrote, "by exceedingly cheerful white men who menaced us with not the faintest scowl and who wore their Ku Klux Klan insignia on the sidebars of their eyeglasses."

Another disturbing fact Baldwin quickly discovered was that whites who committed crimes of racial violence were still treated very lightly. After the jury ruled the defendant guilty, the judge gave the man a 10-year suspended sentence. The accused walked out of the courtroom "free as lightning," according to Baldwin. "Dark Days," his essay on his trip through the South, was published in the October 1980 issue of *Esquire*.

During the 1980s, Baldwin frequently changed his residence, living sometimes in France and sometimes in the United States. In 1981, he returned to

ST. JOHN PARISH (COUNTY) LIBRARY
LAPLACE, LOUISIANA 70068

Baldwin speaks with Myrlie Evers, the widow of Medgar Evers, at a 1983 screening of a television documentary about the slain civil rights leader. The last literary project on which Baldwin worked was a book about Evers, the Reverend Martin Luther King, Jr., and Malcolm X.

the South, this time to cover a sensational murder trial for *Playboy* magazine. The trial, which was popularly called the Atlanta child murder case, concerned the disappearance of 28 black children in Atlanta, Georgia. It was feared that all of the children had been murdered.

In June 1981, a black man named Wayne Williams went on trial for the murders. One month later, he was found guilty of two of the deaths. The court proceedings left many questions unanswered, however, because the evidence brought before the jury never clearly linked all 28 murders to Williams.

Baldwin used the trial as a focal point for his observations about the South. His essay on the murder case, "The Evidence of Things Not Seen," was originally published in the December 1981 issue of *Playboy*; in 1986, it appeared in book form. A searing commentary on America's still-troubled race relations, Baldwin's acccount contained some dark thoughts about the future of Western civilization. "This civilization has proven itself capable of destroying peoples rather than hear them, destroying continents rather than share them, and is capable, for the same reason, of destroying all life on this planet," he wrote.

Baldwin also taught writing at several American colleges during the 1980s. Among the schools where he worked as a writer-in-residence were Bowling Green State University in Bowling Green, Ohio; Morehouse College in Atlanta; and Hampshire College and the University of Massachusetts in Amherst, Massachusetts. He found teaching to be a rewarding experience, and he enjoyed the opportunity to discuss new ideas with his students in debates that often lasted for hours.

In between teaching stints, Baldwin returned to his quiet farmhouse in France, the country he had

Baldwin in 1985, examining a new edition of Go Tell It on the Mountain *at an outdoor café in St. Paul de Vence. His long love affair with France reached a peak one year later, when the French government awarded him its medal of the Legion of Honor.*

Few writers have argued for racial understanding as powerfully as Baldwin. "The terms," he said, "of our revolution—the American revolution—are these: not that I drive you out or that you drive me out, but that we learn to live together."

come to regard as his second home. In 1964, Baldwin was elected to America's prestigious National Institute of Arts and Letters; 22 years later, the French government awarded him one of its highest honors: the medal of the Legion of Honor. Baldwin was the second black American ever to receive the distinction, the first being Josephine Baker, the celebrated blues singer who spent much of her career in Paris. In awarding the medal to Baldwin in 1986, French president François Mitterand said admiringly of his work that it "explains the essential."

For Baldwin, the award amounted to an official embrace from the country he had adopted years earlier. "It's a love affair," he remarked. "I learned a lot in France. This is the place where I grew up, insofar as you can ever say you grow up."

It is fitting that the country that served as a haven for Baldwin turned out to be the place where he spent his final days. He was at his farmhouse in St. Paul de Vence on December 1, 1987, when he died from cancer at the age of 63. Found near him in his room was a manuscript on which he had been working: a study of Malcolm X, Medgar Evers, and the Reverend Martin Luther King, Jr.

Like these fallen civil rights activists, Baldwin remained a champion of the poor and the oppressed until his death. "I want to be an honest man and a good writer," he had said in 1955, and he lived up to that resolve long after he had won fame and riches. Indeed, he was not one to act otherwise.

"I know whence I came and I know how I got here," Baldwin said. "It wasn't because my countrymen loved my big brown eyes." The reason for his appeal was much more obvious: He was a native son. "I love America more than any country in the world," he wrote in the preface to his first book of essays, "and exactly for this reason, I insist on the right to criticize her perpetually."

And criticize her he did—passionately, humorously, relentlessly. His honesty sometimes earned him enemies, but it never failed him as a writer. For James Baldwin, candor and craft always went hand in hand.

APPENDIX

BOOKS BY JAMES BALDWIN

1953 *Go Tell It on the Mountain*

1955 *Notes of a Native Son*

1956 *Giovanni's Room*

1961 *Nobody Knows My Name: More Notes of a Native Son*

1962 *Another Country*

1963 *The Fire Next Time*

1964 *Blues for Mister Charlie* (play); *Nothing Personal* (with Richard Avedon)

1965 *Going to Meet the Man*

1968 *The Amen Corner* (play); *Tell Me How Long the Train's Been Gone*

1969 *Black Anti-Semitism and Jewish Racism*

1971 *A Rap on Race* (with Margaret Mead)

1972 *No Name in the Street; One Day When I Was Lost*

1973 *A Dialogue* (with Nikki Giovanni)

1974 *If Beale Street Could Talk*

1976 *The Devil Finds Work*

1979 *Just Above My Head*

1986 *The Evidence of Things Not Seen*

CHRONOLOGY

1924   Born James Arthur Baldwin in Harlem, New York, on August 2

1930   Enters Public School 24

1937   Becomes editor in chief of *Douglass Pilot* at Frederick Douglass Junior High School

1938   Becomes a preacher at Fireside Pentacostal Assembly

1942   Graduates from De Witt Clinton High School

1943   Moves to Greenwich Village in New York

1944   Wins the Eugene F. Saxton Memorial Trust Award

1945   First book review is published

1948   First major essay, "The Harlem Ghetto," is published; wins a Julius Rosenwald fellowship; moves to Paris

1953   First novel, *Go Tell It on the Mountain,* is published

1955   First book of nonfiction, *Notes of a Native Son,* is published

1956   Baldwin wins a Partisan Review fellowship and the National Institute of Arts and Letters Award

1957   Returns to New York; makes first trip to the South and meets the Reverend Martin Luther King, Jr.

1962   Meets with Elijah Muhammad

1963   *The Fire Next Time* is published; meets with U.S. Attorney General Robert F. Kennedy

1964   Baldwin elected to the National Institute of Arts and Letters

1979   Revisits the South as a journalist

1986   Receives the Legion of Honor from the French government

1987   Dies in St. Paul de Vence, France, on December 1

FURTHER READING

Baker, Houston A., Jr. *Black Literature in America.* New York: McGraw-Hill, 1971.

Bloom, Harold, ed. *James Baldwin.* New York: Chelsea House, 1986.

Davis, Arthur P. *From the Dark Tower: Afro-American Writers, 1900 to 1960.* Washington, DC: Howard University Press, 1982.

Eckman, Fern Marja. *The Furious Passage of James Baldwin.* New York: Popular Library, 1967.

Hassan, Ihab. *Radical Innocence.* Princeton, NJ: Princeton University Press, 1961.

Hill, Herbert, ed. *Anger and Beyond: The Negro Writer in the United States.* New York: Harper & Row, 1966.

Kinnamon. Kenneth. (comp.) *James Baldwin.* Englewood Cliffs, NJ: Prentice-Hall, 1974.

Macebuh, Stanley. *James Baldwin: A Critical Study.* New York: The Third Press, 1973.

O'Daniel, Therman B. *James Baldwin: A Critical Evaluation.* Washington, DC: Howard University Press, 1977.

Pratt, Louis H. *James Baldwin.* Boston: G. K. Hall, 1978.

Sylvander, Carol Wedin. *James Baldwin.* New York: Frederick Ungar, 1980.

INDEX

PICTURE CREDITS

———— ❦ ————

AP/Wide World Photos: pp. 10, 13, 14, 15, 37, 39, 46, 53, 64, 65, 67, 70–71, 72, 73, 76, 77, 81, 90, 96–97, 102, 104; The Beacon Press: p. 54; The Bettmann Archive: pp. 34–35, 40; Culver Pictures: p. 18; Library of Congress: pp. 24, 75, 79, 82; Moorland-Spingarn Research Center, Howard University: pp. 51, 99; New York Public Library: pp. 21, 23, 43, 68; New York Public Library, Astor, Lenox and Tilden Foundations: pp. 16, 22, 30–31; Reuters/Bettmann Newsphotos: p. 103; Robert Sengstacke: pp. 84–85; Ira N. Toff: p. 49; UPI/Bettmann Newsphotos: pp. 12, 19, 26, 32, 56, 59, 61, 62, 86, 89, 93, 94

LISA ROSSET received a B.A. in government from Smith College and an M.A. in international affairs from Columbia University. She has contributed articles to various newspapers and magazines including the *Village Voice*, the *Boston Phoenix*, *Small Press Magazine*, and *Kirkus Reviews*. Formerly an editor for Grove Press, she is now a free-lance editor and writer living in New York City.

NATHAN IRVIN HUGGINS is W.E.B. Du Bois Professor of History and Director of the W.E.B. Du Bois Institute for Afro-American Research at Harvard University. He previously taught at Columbia University. Professor Huggins is the author of numerous books, including *Black Odyssey: The Afro-American Ordeal in Slavery*, *The Harlem Renaissance*, and *Slave and Citizen: The Life of Frederick Douglass*.